LOVE

For that happy band of cousins:

Jennifer, Kirsten, Fiona, Adam, Kingsley, Katherine, Mitchell, Lauren, Courteney, Gael, Ewan, Neil and Chelsea

LOVE HURTS

The Heart of the Christian Story

ALAN SPENCE

19 18 17 16 15 14 13   7 6 5 4 3 2 1

First published 2013 by Paternoster
Paternoster is an imprint of Authentic Media Limited
52 Presley Way, Crownhill, Milton Keynes, MK8 0ES.
www.authenticmedia.co.uk

British Library Cataloguing in Publication Data
A catalogue record for this book is available from the British Library
ISBN 978-1-84227-810-9

Cover Design Phil Houghton
Printed and bound by CPI Group (UK) Ltd., Croydon, CR0 4YY

Contents

Contents

Contents

Preface

Some months back, I was given a copy of Rob Bell's book *Love Wins*. I was fascinated by it. That someone could write with so easy a style while dealing with such important religious ideas was an eye-opener. Perhaps I have been somewhat trapped in a way of thinking which assumed that fairly technical language was necessary to handle the really big issues about God and salvation. I admired the way Bell was able to use humour and provocative questions to encourage ordinary Christians to think through certain key ideas of their faith in quite new ways. I found myself a little envious of his skill as a communicator.

Although I share some of Bell's perspectives and concerns, the answers that I would give to a number of the questions that he raises are rather different. His engaging manner stimulated me to think through my own position more clearly. I soon realized, however, that many of the issues are interrelated and can't be adequately dealt with on their own. Like a single-arch suspension bridge, all of the struts are dependent on one another. In order to explain the forces on any one of them, you need to look at the whole structure. And so I thought it would be more helpful to put together a coherent, alternative account of the Christian story rather than consider piecemeal each of the issues he raised.

My plan was to use the idea of the love of God, which had played such a pivotal role in Bell's presentation, as a guide for my own study. I would examine how the New Testament writers employed the concept of God's love as a key to open up the central features of the Christian message. As for style, I felt that I could at least make an attempt to say things as simply as possible. In particular, I would seek to do so without reference to any theological authorities. For someone who has spent quite a bit of time reading Christian theologians, it is quite a challenge to put them all to one side and be guided only by what the Bible has to say on the matter.

This short book has now been written and I am in a position to look back and take stock. It stands on its own as a fresh presentation of what might be called a classical understanding of the Christian story. It shouldn't be viewed as a direct response to anyone else's work. On a personal note, I discovered that reflecting deeply on the themes of the gospel soon had me captivated by its charms. I found myself humbled by its penetrating insights and I sensed once more the freedom of its liberating power. The apostle Paul once said that we carry this treasure in earthen jars. My hope is that the reader might, like an expensive camera, be able to focus not on the clay jar, but on the treasure that it seeks to bear. And that through such focal attention, he or she might also be drawn to its beauty and persuaded by its logic.

My special thanks to those who read the chapters as they were being written and helped me to improve the text. These include my friend Henriette, my nephew Adam, my wife Sheila and our passionate little theological group at Abington Avenue.

1.

COSTLY LOVE

Asking Questions

What is the heart of the Christian story?
What does it promise?
Does it make any sense?
Is it believable?
What does it ask from me?

For the person thinking seriously about Christianity, these are some of the key issues. The answers, however, are not always clear-cut. Our most important questions often produce a bewildering variety of responses. How are we to decide between them? Everything seems to depend on which group of Christians we ask. Different churches tend to give different answers. Even within the same church, people do not always seem to agree. How does someone who is looking for the truth decide what to believe?

Almost all Christians recognize that the Scriptures have one way or another played an important role in shaping what they hold to be true. If the Bible is the foundational document of the Christian faith, it makes sense to turn first to its pages and consider the answers they offer to questions such as these. The problem, however, as everyone knows, is that people interpret the Scriptures differently. Their experience of life shapes their spirituality. And their spirituality colours their reading of the Bible. Our backgrounds subtly influence the way we view its message. They help us determine what is significant and what is secondary. Our worldview unconsciously fashions our judgement and organizes our filters. None of us comes to the biblical narrative with a completely blank sheet of paper or a totally open mind. Consciously or unconsciously we have already formed a set of answers to the questions we are asking. Perhaps the best we can do is to make a deliberate effort to allow the ideas and perspectives of the Scriptures to speak for themselves, to order their own priorities and to disclose their own agenda.

Another difficulty we are faced with when we read the Bible is to know where to start. It is easy to be overwhelmed by the richness of its teaching and the open-ended nature of its stories. We can often miss the wood for the trees. Are there certain themes about salvation which are the foundation for more peripheral ideas? Are there some stepping-stones that are secure enough for us to place our weight on before we choose to wade out further? Many have held that the love of God lies at the very heart of the Christian story. It sounds like a good call. Let's start there and see where the path leads.

God's Love

Love connects people. It is the life-force of our best relationships. A world without it presents an extremely bleak prospect. Who would choose to live in a loveless relationship? Love is creative. It energizes our poetry, our literature and our music. It is the driving power behind many of our noblest achievements. Love is exhilarating and transforming. It has its own inner strength. It is difficult, if not impossible, to bring it under any sort of control. It cannot be priced. A love poem in the Bible appears to be right on the mark:

Many waters cannot quench love;
rivers cannot sweep it away.
If one were to give
all the wealth of one's house for love,
it would be utterly scorned (Song 8:7).

Love can, however, be made cheap and dirty. It can be used as an advertising tool and a way to control others. Love can be so sentimental that it becomes sickening, like too much sugar in a good cup of coffee. We find caricatures of love in bad movies, corny song lyrics and cheap romantic fiction. When a pop singer shouts out to fifty thousand adoring fans, 'I love you all', what does he mean? Love can be trivialized.

What about God's love for us? How robust a concept is it? How well does it stand up to our attempts to hijack it for our own purposes or flavour it to our own taste? Let us look at some of the principal statements in the New Testament on the nature of God's love for the world:

> For God so loved the world that he gave his one and only Son, that whoever believes in him shall not perish but have eternal life (John 3:16).

> But God demonstrates his own love for us in this: while we were still sinners, Christ died for us (Rom. 5:8).

> This is how God showed his love among us: he sent his one and only Son into the world that we might live through him. This is love: not that we loved God, but that he loved us and sent his Son as an atoning sacrifice for our sins (1 John 4:9,10).

God's love, according to these texts, is made known in the giving over of his Son to death. It is in a particular, concrete, historical event that took place in a minor Roman province some time back that we discover what God's love actually means. We do not learn about God's love by trying to analyze him. It is not rationally deduced from the idea of God. Nor is it derived from our personal reflection on how well life has turned out for us or how beautiful the world appears to be. God's love has to do with the giving over of his Son to death. That's it. Any explanation of divine love which does not flow from our reflection on that supreme gift is in danger of either intellectual abstraction or superficiality and sentimentality.

In the Second World War my dad, his brother-in-law and his younger brother were all pilots in the Royal Air Force. Dad crashed in enemy territory and was taken prisoner for four years. His brother-in-law was killed in action. His younger brother was shot down in air combat and lost at sea in the English Channel, having been seen by a fellow pilot climbing into his life raft. The war clearly cost my grandmother a great deal. But it was the loss of this her youngest child that appeared to grieve her most.

Year after year she continued to insist to her family that there was a chance that her missing son might one day return. Perhaps he had been captured and taken prisoner to East Germany and then at the end of the war had been transferred to Russia. Who knows? Surely it was still possible, even twenty years later, that he might one day simply knock on the door of the family home and call out, 'Mum, I'm home.'

Is God's loss of his Son anything like our loss of a child? Philosophers would generally say no. They would argue that if God is self-sufficient and totally satisfied in himself, then what happens in his own created world cannot cause him any pain. He is unable to be hurt as we are hurt. It is of course true that God is quite different from us. However, we have to be careful not to allow theories about God's unknowability or otherness to undermine the theme of divine love that shapes the Bible story. Time and again, the gospels give particular emphasis to the loving relation between the Father and the Son:

And a voice from heaven said, 'This is my Son, whom I love; with him I am well pleased' (Matt. 3:17).

The Father loves the Son and has placed everything in his hands (John 3:35).

Father, I want those you have given me to be with me where I am, and to see my glory, the glory you have given me because you loved me before the creation of the world (John 17:24).

The writers of the New Testament stress that the love the Father has for Jesus is the springboard for so much else that needs to be said about him. It is significant that the account of God's gift of his only Son is told in a way that reminds us of the story of Abraham offering up his son Isaac as a sacrifice: 'Then God said, "Take your son, your only son, whom you love – Isaac – and go to the region of Moriah. Sacrifice him there as a burnt offering on a mountain that I will show you"' (Gen. 22:2).

It is difficult to understand why this disturbing story, often described within Judaism as 'the binding of Isaac', has had such a prominent place in Jewish literature and art – or for that matter, why it should have so shaped the Christian story. The people of Israel had always considered child sacrifice to be the most terrible of crimes. Of all the evils of pagan religion this was by far the worst. The account of Abraham walking with his son up to Mount Moriah so that he might sacrifice him there is one which causes every caring parent to shudder with horror. It is hardly the sort of bedtime reading one would choose for the children! Yet as dark as the story is, Jews have returned to it repeatedly for reflection and inspiration. Some have recognized in the obedience displayed there the noblest acts of their martyrs. The New Testament has interpreted Abraham's action as an indication of the reality of his faith. He has learnt that the divine promise can never fail. Isaac will live whatever happens. Søren Kierkegaard, the Danish philosopher, understood Abraham's obedience to point to the radical nature of our unconditional response to God.

We see, then, that the Bible describes God's love as the love that is made known in the Father's gift of his Son. It is told in a way which indicates that it was both costly and painful. Loving the world was not, for God, simply an attitude or a disposition. It was an action which cost him dearly.

What does it mean to take this perspective seriously in our interpretation of the Christian story? Well, other theories about the significance of God's love have to be moved to the wings if this one is allowed to take centre stage. Let me explain. A popular theory today is that God's love for the world is shown in his decision to share in its deepest sufferings. We are not left alone in our trials. God has identified with our pain through the life and death of Jesus. Another idea is that God's love is the power by which he overcomes the forces of darkness. Love is the real source of his ultimate victory over evil.

Now, it is of course true that Jesus participated fully in the sufferings and temptations of humankind. And it is also rightly said that God, through the life and death of Christ, has triumphed over evil. The point, however, is that when the Scriptures speak about the love of God, these are not the issues that they highlight. We can of course co-opt the idea of the 'love of God' for agendas such as these. But when we do so, we are no longer allowing the biblical narrative to speak for itself, to emphasize its own priorities, to tell its own story.

The Love of the Son

How does the idea that God's love is made known in the gift of his Son fashion the Christian story? In the first place, it shapes the way we are to understand Christ's own love for the world. Jesus demonstrates his love for us by the free surrender of his own life:

> This is how we know what love is: Jesus Christ laid down his life for us. And we ought to lay down our lives for our brothers and sisters (1 John 3:16).

> I live by faith in the Son of God, who loved me and gave himself for me (Gal. 2:20b).

> Husbands, love your wives, just as Christ loved the church and gave himself up for her (Eph. 5:25)

> Greater love has no one than this: to lay down one's life for one's friends (John 15:13).

Now, this idea that Jesus freely gave up his life for us as an act of love does, of course, undermine other ways of interpreting his death. Some would see Jesus' crucifixion as the execution of one of society's powerless by the religious and military powers of the world. But although that is undoubtedly true, it is not the most significant thing that can be said about his execution by the Romans. Jesus' death was the outcome of his own decision. The gospels insist that Christ gave his life freely. It was not taken from him: 'The reason my Father loves me is that I lay down my life – only to take it up again. No one takes it from me, but I lay it down of my own accord' (John 10:17,18).

There is no suggestion that this was an easy choice. Jesus' impending death was for him a dark cloud that overshadowed his long journey to Jerusalem. During hours of lonely anguish in prayer in Gethsemane, he finally came to terms with it. But it was, nevertheless, his free choice. Judas betrayed him. The trial by the Sanhedrin was rigged. From start to finish it was a cynical miscarriage of justice. Pilate showed himself to be a moral coward by washing his hands of all responsibility. Jesus was mocked by Roman guards and nailed to the cross with Roman nails. Everyone seems to have played some part in killing him. But the biblical narrative insists that Jesus' death flowed out of a choice that had already been made. He himself had made his fateful decision on the Mount of Olives the night before. And we have to take that seriously. His death was to be an act of his love, freely given.

This sort of love is costly.

It was costly for the Father.

It was costly for the Son.

And we too will experience something of that cost if we follow him faithfully and learn to love in his way.

Summary

Let me consider what these early steps in our reflection on God's love might mean for the Christian story. The death of Christ is to be presented as an act of love towards us, a love of both the Father and the Son. The two cannot be easily separated. To explain the cross in a way which highlighted the love of the one and not the other would be to distort the gospel message. The Father gives up his Son to death. He does so at great cost. In doing so, he demonstrates his love for the world. The Son in obedience to his Father freely surrenders his life in his love for his fellows. The New Testament writers manage to hold together both of these ideas. Neither takes priority.

This emphasis on the love of the Father and the Son suggests that the story of the cross is, at least in part, an address to our emotions. In the academic or business world, expressions of love add nothing to the force of an argument. But the death of Jesus has to do with our world of relations, particularly our relationship with God. And in that world, love is the most powerful of forces. The gospel is at its heart a love story. This is why it is both exciting and scary. On the one hand we long for love. On the other we are terrified by the commitment that it demands.

The cross is a declaration of divine love towards us. We are invited to recognize ourselves as the object of that love. For the person who has not become hardened to such a possibility, the realization that they are the focus of such affection can be for them the cause of wonder and astonishment, of liberation and delight. Like someone receiving a Valentine card, they are eager to find out more about the one who sent it.

Who, then, is Jesus? We have described him in this chapter as the Son of God and spoken of God as his Father, suggesting that they have some sort of particularly close relationship. Perhaps the time has come to try and unpack these terms and say what we mean by them.

2.

HIS ONLY SON

For God so loved the world that he gave his one and only Son
(John 3:16).

Why is Jesus described in the New Testament as God's one and
only Son? What does this mean?

When you come to think about it, the whole Christian story seems
to depend on the answer given to these questions. Everything that
is distinctive about the Christian faith is closely related to the person of Jesus and what is involved in him being the Son of God. Our
view of his person has shaped the way we understand who God is,
how we come to salvation and what is our own future.

I have some friends who strongly disagree with me on this.
They argue that it is what Jesus said and did that is important,
not who he is. They believe that in this matter the church has been
an unwitting part of an enormous, global scam. It has clothed a
humble Galilean preacher with robes of glory and honour that
would surely have been a great embarrassment to him. They say
that it would be much better if we listened to what Jesus taught
and followed his way of life, rather than spend our time treating
him as some sort of divine being.

Talking with them, I have begun to realize how difficult it is for
men and women who hold such views to remain in the church with
integrity. From their perspective almost everything that Christians
do in their services of worship has the appearance of blasphemy.
We honour Jesus as divine in our hymns. We pray through Jesus
to the Father in our intercessions. We share in a meal that Jesus
invites us to, eating bread and drinking wine as symbols of his
body and blood. We bless one another in his name as we go out

into the world. We solemnly stand together and recite a statement
of shared belief which leaves little room for misunderstanding:

> We believe in one Lord, Jesus Christ,
> the only Son of God,
> eternally begotten of the Father,
> God from God, Light from Light,
> true God from true God,
> begotten, not made,
> of one Being with the Father.[1]

In all of this, one thing appears to be absolutely clear. Christians
do take the question of who Jesus is very seriously indeed. It is
not possible to neatly sidestep the discussion about his person.
If we are interested in the essence of the Christian story, we need
to hear what the New Testament writers have to say about who
Jesus is.

The First Real Human

Telling stories about various encounters that Jesus had in his
ministry appears to have played a key role in much early Christian preaching. Within a few years these narratives were brought
together to form the first gospel, probably Mark's. The gospel
wasn't like a modern biography offering a chronological account
of someone's whole life. It was rather dozens of short stories that
had been used in evangelism and teaching, now woven together
to present an ordered account of Jesus' three years of ministry,
with a particular focus on all that had happened around the time
of his death. Matthew and Luke added narratives of the events
surrounding Jesus' birth and resurrection along with collections
of Jesus' sayings, but the basic pattern remained much the same.
These gospels, along with that of John, provide our basic source
material for Jesus' life. What do they tell us about his person?

They describe a young Jewish teacher or rabbi who was widely
recognized across the region as a healer and worker of miracles.
The power of God's Spirit was apparent in his life and it characterized his ministry. It gave clear shape to his personal sense of calling:

The Spirit of the Lord is upon me,
> because the Lord has anointed me.

He has sent me to preach good news to the poor,
> to proclaim release to the prisoners
> and recovery of sight to the blind,
> to liberate the oppressed,
> and to proclaim the year of the Lord's favour (Luke 4:18,19 CEB).

This understanding of Jesus as a man empowered by God is summarized in Peter's sermon on the day of Pentecost: 'Jesus of Nazareth was a man accredited by God to you by miracles, wonders and signs, which God did among you through him, as you yourselves know' (Acts 2:22). The significance of this interpretation is that the miracles that Jesus performed were seen as an indication of the Spirit's presence in his life and are a witness to his particular mission, as the long-promised Messiah, to bring in the kingdom of God. They, of themselves, do not indicate that he is divine: 'But if it is by the Spirit of God that I drive out demons, then the kingdom of God has come upon you' (Matt. 12:28). Further, the mighty deeds done by Jesus in the power of the Spirit are in no way substantially different from the possibilities that are open to his followers: 'Very truly I tell you, whoever believes in me will do the works I have been doing, and they will do even greater things than these, because I am going to the Father' (John 14:12).

The New Testament writers indicate that Jesus was totally dependent on God. There is perhaps nothing that shows this more clearly than his life of prayer. The more significant the decisions that needed to be made, the more urgently he called to his Father for guidance and strength: 'During the days of Jesus' life on earth, he offered up prayers and petitions with fervent cries and tears to the one who could save him from death, and he was heard because of his reverent submission' (Heb. 5:7).

The Scriptures argue that Jesus was like us in every way. The only difference was that he lived without sin. He was tempted as we are tempted. He came into our world alongside us and shared in its pain, frustration and suffering. He sought in all things to do the Father's will and eventually found himself being crushed in doing so. He stood as a man before God, in no way different from us. He had a body like ours and a brain that operated in the same way that ours does. He was part of a religious culture and world that shaped his life and his thinking. How he acted and spoke can be understood in the light of the world in which he lived and the beliefs he held. Put bluntly, there are no tools available in the physical, social or historical sciences that could ever establish that this man was more than human.

Jesus was human in the same way that we are, but without the damaging and dehumanizing effects of sin, its fears and addictions, its self-delusions and pretensions. We could say he was the first really human person to walk this planet ever since our original parents lost the plot and turned against their Maker. He is the model for how we might now live. He is the pattern of our new humanity.

An Opening of Eyes

Followers of Jesus, including members of his own family, came to believe that this way of understanding him, although true, was inadequate. It told only half the story. He was not simply a man like us. When their eyes were opened by the Spirit, they came to see more clearly who he really was. This is how it happened to Peter:

> When Jesus came to the region of Caesarea Philippi, he asked his disciples, 'Who do people say the Son of Man is?'
>
> They replied, 'Some say John the Baptist; others say Elijah; and still others, Jeremiah or one of the prophets.'
>
> 'But what about you?' he asked. 'Who do you say I am?'
>
> Simon Peter answered, 'You are the Messiah, the Son of the living God.'
>
> Jesus replied, 'Blessed are you, Simon son of Jonah, for this was not revealed to you by flesh and blood, but by my Father in heaven' (Matt. 16:13–17).

Later the disciple Thomas, who had been so full of doubt, recognized who Jesus really was when he saw the risen Christ standing before him. He immediately offered him divine worship (see John 20:26–28). A similar revelatory event happened to Paul on the way to Damascus (see Acts 9:1–19). It generally seems to have been their engagement with his resurrection, along with the ascension and outpouring of the Spirit, which enabled the early disciples to reach this 'dual' view of Jesus: '[The gospel] is about his Son: on the human level he was born of David's stock, but on the level of the spirit – the Holy Spirit – he was declared Son of God by a mighty act in that he rose from the dead' (Rom. 1:3,4 NEB).

That a community of Jewish monotheists should cross over this boundary marker of their faith and begin to offer divine worship to a fellow Jew is quite incredible. Equally difficult for us to understand is the fact that the early Christian church appears to have had no internal debate about this. In their hymns and benedictions all our sources indicate that Jesus was universally honoured just as God was honoured. The New Testament outlines a series of events which lay behind this quite amazing development.

The prophetic ministry of John the Baptist and the preaching and healing ministry of Jesus had fuelled the expectation of many pious Jews in Judea and Galilee that the coming kingdom of God was about to appear. The announcement of Jesus' resurrection after he had been executed by the Romans, along with the public outpouring of the Holy Spirit on the early disciples, was a clear sign to the faithful that the promised divine kingdom – already visible in the signs, wonders and miracles of Jesus' ministry – was finally breaking into the present age. It was with these things in mind that many responded positively to Peter's presentation of the gospel on the Day of Pentecost. They were baptized for the forgiveness of their sins and, receiving the promised Holy Spirit, they experienced the salvation of God. The announcement that Jesus had been raised to a position of authority at the right hand of God was confirmed by their own dramatic experience of the Spirit, a proof for them that Jesus was indeed now at God's right hand, crowned as King. In such a situation it is not so difficult to understand why these early disciples felt it was totally appropriate to offer divine worship to the risen, exalted Christ.

But how did a community steeped in monotheism make sense of all this? What theological explanation did it give for Jesus' person?

A Pre-existent Being

In one of the earliest Christian writings there is a suggestion of an already existing hymn with these lines:

> Though he was in the form of God,
> > he did not consider being equal with God something to exploit.
> But he emptied himself
> > by taking the form of a slave
> > and by becoming like human beings.
> When he found himself in the form of a human,
> > he humbled himself by becoming obedient to the point of death,
> > even death on a cross.
> Therefore, God highly honoured him
> > and gave him a name above all names,
> so that at the name of Jesus everyone
> > in heaven, on earth, and under the earth might bow
> > and every tongue confess that Jesus Christ is Lord, to the glory
> > of God the Father (Phil. 2:6–11 CEB).

It would seem that as far back as our source material takes us, we find Christians believing that a person who was equal to God had humbled himself and taken human form. It was in due course argued that this pre-existent person had in recent history become enfleshed or incarnated as a man. He became a truly human person: 'The Word became flesh and made his dwelling among us. We have seen his glory, the glory of the one and only Son, who came from the Father, full of grace and truth' (John 1:14). And this is one of the conceptual ways in which the early Christians held together the dual perspective on Jesus. Existing with God from the beginning of time, he had now been incarnated as a man.

This idea of the Son's pre-existence is suggested in all those sayings which speak of him as having seen God, or come from God, or being sent by God: 'No one has ever seen God, but the one and only Son, who is himself God and is in the closest relationship with the Father, has made him known' (John 1:18). We are now hopefully in a better position to understand what it means to speak of Jesus as the only Son of God.

The One and Only Son

The New Testament writers used the term 'Son' with reference to Jesus to distinguish him from all other prophets or servants of God:

> In the past God spoke to our ancestors through the prophets at many times and in various ways, but in these last days he has spoken to us by his Son, whom he appointed heir of all things, and through whom also he made the universe. The Son is the radiance of God's glory and the exact representation of his being, sustaining all things by his powerful word (Heb. 1:1–3).

Moses, that supreme instrument of divine revelation and spiritual authority in the Jewish religion, is considered to belong to a completely different category to Jesus: 'Jesus has been found worthy of greater honour than Moses, just as the builder of a house has greater honour than the house itself . . . Moses was faithful as a servant in all God's house, bearing witness to what would be spoken by God in the future. But Christ is faithful as the Son over God's house' (Heb. 3:3,5,6). Jesus is the builder of God's house, not just a part of it. He is a son, not merely a servant. He is the heir to all that God has. He is the radiance of God's glory, the exact representation of his being. He is the image of the invisible God, and all of God's fullness dwells in him. This is what it means to the authors of the New Testament for Jesus to be God's only Son. He is worthy of all the honour that is due to the Father (see John 5:23). And this willingness to honour him is reflected in the hymns of God's people in heaven, even as it is on earth:

> 'Worthy is the Lamb, who was slain,
>> to receive power and wealth and wisdom and strength
>> and honour and glory and praise!'

> Then I heard every creature in heaven and on earth and under the earth and on the sea, and all that is in them, saying:

> 'To him who sits on the throne and to the Lamb
>> be praise and honour and glory and power,
>> for ever and ever!' (Rev. 5:12,13).

If we want to know who has come to us with a declaration of his love, this is he – the Son of God. It is the Father of this Son who has made known his love for the world by giving him up to death. Equally it is this Son of the Father who has loved us enough to die for us.

But why was it done? What was the point?

A boy burns his arm with a cigarette to prove to his girl that he loves her. But surely this sort of meaningless demonstration of love does not help us to understand why Jesus gave up his life. There has to be a reason.

Why was it, then, that the Father handed over his only Son to death?

3.

IN PRAISE OF JUSTICE

They Shall Not Perish

It can be frustrating when you ask a thoughtful person an interesting question and a somewhat opinionated bystander leans forward and answers on their behalf. Wanting to hear what they have to say, you find yourself asking the same question again, more pointedly perhaps, hoping that this time they will be given a chance to speak for themselves.

We have been considering some of the principal texts on the love of God in the New Testament, and we are, as it were, asking questions of them. We want to hear them speak for themselves. Our questions are simple: Why did the Father give his Son over to death? Why did the Son choose to die? The answer they give appears to be equally straightforward. It was, at least in part, so that we might not perish: 'For God so loved the world that he gave his one and only Son, that whoever believes in him shall not perish but have eternal life' (John 3:16).

Some have understood 'perishing' in this verse to refer to human ageing. Our bodies are mortal. Try as we might, we cannot halt the process that leads us inevitably towards old age and death. The good news is that God has become mortal to make us immortal. The grave no longer has the final word. God gave over his Son to death so that we might live forever.

The problem with such an interpretation is that the context of the passage we are considering indicates something quite different about the nature of the human predicament – about the meaning of perishing. Our plight as outlined in this chapter has to do not with ageing or dying physically but with coming under divine judgement: 'Whoever believes in him is not condemned, but whoever does not believe stands condemned already because they have not believed in the name of God's one and only Son . . . Whoever believes in the Son has eternal life, but whoever rejects the Son will not see life, for God's wrath remains on them' (John 3:18,36).

God's wrath needs to be understood here not as the uncontrolled, emotional outburst of a divine being who has lost his temper, but rather as the considered judicial sentence of a just God against that which is evil. It is a decision which flows from the holiness of his person. Divine judgement is not a theme that sits particularly easily with our modern religious understanding. We have all sorts of difficulties with the notion of God judging us and so it is our natural instinct to shy away from these ideas when we find them in the Scriptures. We tend to block them out and move on to other, more positive topics. But let's stop for a moment and consider a little more closely the concept of judgement and its relation to justice. To help focus our minds, let me outline a situation which sadly could happen almost anywhere.

The Nature of Judgement

You hold a position of responsibility in the church. One day, the much loved minister of a large congregation confesses to you that some years earlier he had sexually interfered with an eleven-year-old girl while she was staying at his home. The girl had recently made the incident known to her own pastor and parents. They insisted he bring the matter to you. What do you do?

Do you pray with him and encourage him that if he faithfully confesses his sin and turns away from it, God will be merciful and forgive him? And then simply leave it at that?

Do you take the matter to the church authorities, recognizing that the moment you do so, you will have begun a process that will bring incredible suffering on him and sadly on his innocent family? He might never be able to minister again.

Assuming the action becomes a matter of church discipline, should the focus be on his punishment, his restoration or on the protection of other children?

Is there any need to make the matter public? Why?

18

Assuming it is not a requirement of the state, should the police be informed? Why?

What is required for justice to be done? If you were a friend of the minister, you would probably come up with different answers to those given by someone close to the family of the girl who was abused. Perhaps that is why we require our judges to be unacquainted with the parties that come before them. Further, if you were well informed about the terrible damage caused by child abuse, you might ask for a sterner sentence than if you weren't.

Let us stop for a moment and consider what is taking place in the process of making a judgement such as this. I find it helpful to consider the whole event as an act of truth-revealing. First, what actually happened needs to be brought to light. Righteous judgement requires that the covers of darkness be lifted and the truth of the incident be made known. The facts of the matter must be revealed. The truth is important. Its publication brings glory to God even when the deed is dark: 'Then Joshua said to Achan, "My son, give glory to the LORD, the God of Israel, and honour him. Tell me what you have done; do not hide it from me"' (Josh. 7:19).

Second, the appropriate punishment for the offence is itself a revelation of truth. Right punishment makes apparent the proper seriousness of the crime. Let me illustrate. I was deeply angered at one time during a period of armed conflict in my country to discover that the penalty that a soldier received from the military for losing his rifle was harsher than that meted out to him for the unnecessary killing of a civilian child. There is no truth in this ordering of punishment. It is not just. It indicates a terrible distortion of value or worth. Right sentencing is a disclosure of truth. The life of the child is worth infinitely more than the loss of a rifle. And proper judgement or sentencing must reflect that. Good judgement brings about justice.

The Justice of God

It is not only magistrates, judges and those with responsible positions in the church or the military that have to make such judgements. Employers do it, teachers do it, parents do it. Holding positions of responsible authority will generally require us to make some sort of judicial decision on the behaviour of others. They all play a part in effecting justice. What about God? Is he required to act as judge? The Scriptures do not indicate that God created this world and then pulled back from it, but rather that he continues to sustain it faithfully and to govern it righteously. And an essential part of all good government is fair judgement:

> He rules the world in righteousness
> > and judges the peoples with equity (Ps. 9:8).

> Let all creation rejoice before the LORD, for he comes,
> > he comes to judge the earth.
> He will judge the world in righteousness
> > and the peoples in his faithfulness (Ps. 96:13).

> . . . let them sing before the LORD,
> > for he comes to judge the earth.
> He will judge the world in righteousness
> > and the peoples with equity (Ps. 98:9).

One senses as one reads through the wealth of biblical references to God's judgement that his people take great joy in this aspect of his divine sovereignty over the world and glorify their God for it. Instead of being a problem or an embarrassment to them, God's righteous judgements are a reason for celebration. They are the subject matter of their hymns of worship and praise:

> Let the trees of the forest sing,
> > let them sing for joy before the LORD,
> > for he comes to judge the earth (1 Chr. 16:33).

> The LORD reigns for ever;
> > he has established his throne for judgment (Ps. 9:7).

> Mount Zion rejoices,
> > the villages of Judah are glad
> > because of your judgments (Ps. 48:11).

In the face of the corruption of the courts, the bribing of officials and the uncanny ability of the powerful to bend justice to their own ends, the only confidence of the weak, the exploited and the abused is that the Judge of all the earth will do what is right. He will one day bring the truth to light. He is a God who loves justice. It is for them the great glory of God that he is just in all his judgements.

Christ as Judge

But does the New Testament not transform this perspective? Is the view of God as the glorious Judge of all the earth not a particularly Old Testament way of looking at the world? Do things not change with the coming of Jesus? Yes, we must answer. There is a change. Jesus of Nazareth, born of a woman and crucified under Pontius Pilate, has now been appointed as King of the coming kingdom and as the final Judge of both the living and the dead:

> For he has set a day when he will judge the world with justice by the man he has appointed. He has given proof of this to everyone by raising him from the dead (Acts 17:31).

> For we must all appear before the judgment seat of Christ, so that each of us may receive what is due to us for the things done while in the body, whether good or bad (2 Cor. 5:10).

Today many are hesitant to emphasize the justice of God as an important aspect of his character. There is a tendency, rather, to engage with parodies of God's judicial acts and, in ridiculing them, to dismiss the whole notion of divine judgement. It is sometimes implied that God's sentencing is disproportionate to the level of wrongdoing or even that the innocent might suffer under his hand. An earlier age would have rightly regarded such charges as blasphemy. It is the consistent witness of the Scriptures that God is absolutely just in all his judgements. We can trust him to be perfectly fair in everything he does. Further, we can be assured that all who come before him will see plainly that his decisions have been justly made. His judgements show forth the truth. They establish his justice. After the divine sentence is pronounced, heaven itself will respond:

> Yes, Lord God Almighty,
>   true and just are your judgments (Rev. 16:7).

Limited to caricatures of divine judgement, many today also have difficulty in acknowledging Christ's role as the final Judge of humankind. They fail to recognize that it is an integral aspect of his ministry as the true King of the coming kingdom. The scriptural witness, however, is clear. Jesus' appointment as supreme Judge of all the earth is an indication of the high status that the Father has granted him. In fact, we are warned that a failure to honour Jesus in this role dishonours the Father: 'Moreover, the Father judges no one, but has entrusted all judgment to the Son, that all may honour the Son just as they honour the Father. Whoever does not honour the Son does not honour the Father, who sent him' (John 5:22,23).

The young man from Nazareth who suffered a humiliating death at Calvary has now been raised to a position of the highest authority. Jesus' role as Judge becomes for the New Testament church a vital component of the gospel message: 'He commanded us to preach to the people and to testify that he is the one whom God appointed as judge of the living and the dead. All the prophets testify about him that everyone who believes in him receives forgiveness of sins through his name' (Acts 10:42,43).

Justice and Peace

God is a God of justice who is fair in all his judgements. Old and New Testaments bear constant witness to this. Being made in his image, we ourselves are called to seek justice and to rejoice in the justice of God. I must say it has taken me some time to form a positive estimation of divine justice and the place of divine judgement.

In 1980, after a long period of guerrilla warfare, ninety years of white rule was finally brought to an end in Zimbabwe. The two principal militant organizations, ZANU and ZAPU, assumed political power with widespread public approval. Robert Mugabe as leader of ZANU, the larger of the two parties, was democratically elected as prime minister. Over the next few years the country flourished in all sorts of ways. New schools were built; roads into rural areas were paved; rural clinics sprang up everywhere; the economy expanded. White farmers who stayed in the country found that they were making more money than ever before. The one damper on all this good news was the activity of a group of ZAPU dissidents in Matabeleland. They drew attention to their cause by murdering some tourists driving up to the Victoria Falls. Mugabe responded decisively. He used North Korean military advisers to train the notorious 'Fifth Brigade'. The Fifth Brigade was in due course to ruthlessly eliminate all political dissent in the remote Ndebele villages. After this show of strength Mugabe was able to unite both political parties to form ZANU (PF) and create, in effect, a one-party state. The country was now both prosperous and stable.

There was, however, a fly in the ointment. Mike Auret worked in the Catholic Commission for Justice and Peace. I think it is fair to say that he was both an irritant to Mugabe and a cause of continuing embarrassment to the rest of us. Auret was determined to investigate and bring to public knowledge the murder of civilians by the Fifth Brigade in Matabeleland. A number of mass graves had been discovered, but no meaningful investigation into the matter had ever been made by the authorities. It was difficult for most of us to understand what value there could be in opening up these old sores and offending an effective but clearly ruthless prime minister. I found the slogan of Auret's organization, printed on a poster in his office, to be particularly provoking: 'If you want peace, fight for justice.' I was at the time a city councillor in Harare representing ZANU (PF) and was, so to speak, part of the system. But Mike Auret's commitment to the cause of justice played an important role in changing my perspective. I began to sense that the 'good guys', the people on God's side, were those who wanted the truth to be brought into the open. It was the researchers, who walked from village to village asking questions about missing relatives and carefully recording everything they heard, that I now regarded as moral heroes. I had a growing realization that the desire for truth and justice was something that lay very close to the heart of God. I also began to appreciate why those of us who benefited from the current political order were reluctant to do anything that might destabilize it. To preserve peace and prosperity, we were quite content for unpalatable truth to remain forever buried.

A Fresh Look at the Scriptures

It is interesting how a fresh insight of this nature can alter the way we read certain sections of the Bible. Previously unnoticed themes become prominent or significant as our viewpoint changes. I became more aware of concepts like 'the Day of the Lord', a day when Jews expected God's salvation to be expressed in the judgement of evil and in upholding the cause of the righteous:

> For the LORD has a day of vengeance,
> > a year of retribution, to uphold Zion's cause (Isa. 34:8).

One of the tasks of the promised Messiah would be to announce this coming day of salvation, which included judgement and divine vengeance:

> The Spirit of the Sovereign LORD is on me,
> > because the LORD has anointed me
> > to preach good news to the poor.
> He has sent me to bind up the broken-hearted,
> > to proclaim freedom for the captives
> > and release from darkness for the prisoners,
> to proclaim the year of the LORD's favour
> > and the day of vengeance of our God (Isa. 61:1,2).

And this is precisely what Jesus did. In parable after parable, he identified the coming kingdom of God with an act of divine judgement that would separate out the good from the evil:

> The kingdom of heaven is like a man who sowed good seed in his field. But while everyone was sleeping, his enemy came and sowed weeds among the wheat . . . [The owner told his servants,] 'first collect the

24

weeds and tie them in bundles to be burned; then gather the wheat and bring it into my barn' (Matt. 13:24,30).

Once again, the kingdom of heaven is like a net that was let down into the lake and caught all kinds of fish. When it was full, the fishermen pulled it up on the shore. Then they sat down and collected the good fish in baskets, but threw the bad away (Matt. 13:47,48).

When the Son of Man comes in his glory, and all the angels with him, he will sit on his glorious throne. All the nations will be gathered before him, and he will separate the people one from another as a shepherd separates the sheep from the goats (Matt. 25:31,32).

Now, if the announcement of the coming kingdom of God includes the prospect of divine judgement, it is not at all surprising that the people who heard Jesus' words and took them to heart should hurry down to the river Jordan, confess their sins and be baptized. It was as though an amnesty had been declared. What was quite unexpected was the number of Pharisees and Sadducees who joined them. Had they also repented? Why then did their lives not show it? John asked of them, 'Who warned you to flee from the coming wrath?' (Matt. 3:7). His own task was clear. He was to baptize the penitent in the light of the impending judgement of Christ: 'I baptise you with water for repentance. But after me comes one who is more powerful than I, whose sandals I am not worthy to carry. He will baptise you with the Holy Spirit and fire. His winnowing fork is in his hand, and he will clear his threshing-floor, gathering his wheat into the barn and burning up the chaff with unquenchable fire' (Matt. 3:11,12).

For a number of years, I had read passages like this without consciously registering their reference to divine judgement. Mike Auret's personal crusade to expose the Matabeleland atrocities gave me a new appreciation of God's own inherent justice. I came to see that questions of justice and judgement lie at the very heart of the message of the kingdom of God. The murder of innocents, atrocities carried out against children, the exploitation of the weak, the abuse of women, along with the countless other crimes that we commit against one another daily are to be exposed and dealt with effectively at that time. And Jesus has been appointed as King of that coming kingdom.

Summary

It is the glory of God and the ongoing hope of a suffering people that God will be just in all his judgements. All that is evil will finally perish under his hand. For some of us, this is not particularly good news. We recognize ourselves to be those who have exploited the vulnerable and not stood up for the weak. We have used our power and privilege for personal advantage with heartless disregard for those who suffer around us. In short, we are the weeds rather than the wheat, the goats and not the sheep, the foolish virgins rather than those who were wise, builders on the sand rather than builders on the rock. Our past crimes lie buried in shallow unmarked graves and are soon to be opened. We fully deserve to perish under the good and righteous judgement of God.

At the beginning of this chapter the questions were asked: Why did God hand over his only Son to death? Why did Jesus freely surrender his own life for his fellows? The answer from our text is startling, liberating and full of deep mystery. It was so that those who believe in him might not perish under his holy and righteous judgement but rather be granted life eternal.

Amazing! Incomprehensible! Sometimes a response of silence is more appropriate than all our words.

But how can this be? How does the death of Jesus bring about such a situation?

4.

THE MEANS OF FORGIVENESS

How is Jesus' death related to the forgiveness of sin? This must surely rank as one of the most interesting and perplexing questions in all of theology. One of the three verses we have been considering suggests an answer: 'This is how God showed his love among us: He sent his one and only Son into the world that we might live through him. This is love: not that we loved God, but that he loved us and sent his Son as an atoning sacrifice for our sins' (1 John 4:9,10).

Jesus' death is described here as an atoning sacrifice for our sins. The expression 'atoning sacrifice' is the careful attempt by some modern translators to get a grip on the rather slippery Greek word *hilasmos*. If we could grasp precisely what the New Testament writers meant by this expression, we might have an answer to our question. Let us look a little more closely into how the word is used.

Earlier versions of the English Bible translated *hilasmos* as 'propitiation'. However, this is not an expression you are likely to hear in general conversation today. In pagan religion the word referred to human attempts to placate or calm down an angry god. But this idea cannot be applied straightforwardly to the God who has made himself known to Jews and Christians. The God of the Bible is not like an angry bear with a sore head that has to be pacified with red meat. He is the altogether Holy One whose purity is like the fire of the sun, and even angels must shield their eyes from its brightness. God's 'wrath' is generally a way of speaking about his righteous judgement against sin, flowing from the holiness of his person.

A Cry for Mercy

If *hilasmos* is not to be interpreted as calming down or buying off an angry God, what does it mean? Rather than allowing our understanding of the word to be determined by its use in pagan religion, it might be helpful to see how it, and other words like it, were used in the Jewish and Christian Scriptures, or at least in the Greek translation of them. We will need to look a little more closely at some of the biblical texts.

In the face of this coming divine judgement, the word *hilasmos* is sometimes used in the Psalms to refer to the possibility of forgiveness:

> Out of the depths I cry to you, O LORD;
>   O Lord, hear my voice.
> Let your ears be attentive
>   to my cry for mercy.

> If you, O LORD, kept a record of sins,
>   O LORD, who could stand?
> But with you there is forgiveness;
>   therefore you are feared (Ps. 130:1–4 NIV 1984).

Hilasmos is here understood to bring about a change in our standing before God. If God kept a record of our sins, we would not be able to enter his presence. But now, it is suggested, the list of our sins is shredded so that we might worship him or stand in awe of him. The emphasis is on what happens to the way God views our transgressions and therefore on the transformation of our status before him, rather than on any alteration that takes place in God's own emotional state. The message of the early Christians is that, out of his love for us, God has given up his Son to death so that our standing before him might be totally changed. But how does Christ's death transform our status in this way?

To broaden our understanding of the meaning of *hilasmos*, let us consider how words of the same type were used in the course of ordinary life in Jesus' day.

I once had to tell a young man that his attractive 24-year-old wife had been killed in a car crash. After searching the town,

28

I eventually found him in the early hours of the morning at a party with another girl. When he heard about the accident he lay face down on the ground, overcome with grief, remorse and guilt. He was a powerful tough-minded athlete, but he beat the earth with his fists and cried out like an animal in pain. Jesus tells a parable about a man also caught up in the despair of self-condemnation:

> Two men went up to the temple to pray, one a Pharisee and the other a tax collector. The Pharisee stood by himself and prayed: 'God, I thank you that I am not like other people – robbers, evildoers, adulterers – or even like this tax collector. I fast twice a week and give a tenth of all I get.'
>
> But the tax collector stood at a distance. He would not even look up to heaven, but beat his breast and said, 'God, have mercy on me (*hilastheti*), a sinner.'
>
> I tell you that this man, rather than the other, went home justified before God (Luke 18:10–14).

The life-saving cry of the tax collector is for God's forgiveness. He is a broken man. He knows full well that he is deserving of divine judgement. In his deep pain he appeals to the mercy of God. Instead of holy justice he seeks undeserved grace. Instead of death he cries out for life. 'God, be merciful to me, a sinner' is a good translation of the Greek phrase. The tax collector's desire, in technical terms, is that he be moved from a state of condemnation to one of justification, from death to life. God is being called on to receive this man, overwhelmed by sin, as a friend. Describing Jesus' death as *hilasmos* for sins suggests that his crucifixion serves as an effective cry to his Father in heaven to have mercy on those who deserve only judgement.

The Place of Mercy

King David was considered to have too much blood on his hands to build a temple for the LORD in Jerusalem. The task fell to his son Solomon. In Solomon's momentous prayer at its dedication, we catch a glimpse of the proper function of the temple:

When your people Israel have been defeated by an enemy because they have sinned against you, and when they turn back to you and give praise to your name, praying and making supplication to you in this temple, then hear from heaven and forgive the sin of your people Israel and bring them back to the land you gave to their ancestors.

When the heavens are shut up and there is no rain because your people have sinned against you, and when they pray towards this place and give praise to your name and turn from their sin because you have afflicted them, then hear from heaven and forgive the sin of your servants, your people Israel . . .

When famine or plague comes to the land . . . and when a prayer or plea is made by anyone among your people Israel – being aware of the afflictions of their own hearts, and spreading out their hands toward this temple – then hear from heaven, your dwelling-place. Forgive and act . . .

When they sin against you – for there is no one who does not sin – and you become angry with them and give them over to their enemies, who take them captive to their own lands, far away or near; and if they have a change of heart in the land where they are held captive, and repent and plead with you in the land of their captors and say, 'We have sinned, we have done wrong, we have acted wickedly'; and if they turn back to you with all their heart and soul in the land of their enemies who took them captive, and pray to you . . . then from heaven, your dwelling-place, hear their prayer and their plea, and uphold their cause. And forgive your people, who have sinned against you; forgive all the offences they have committed against you, and cause their captors to show them mercy (1 Kgs 8:33–36,37–39,46–50).

The temple in Jerusalem is the place towards which the people were to pray to receive divine mercy. It was the focal point for their prayers to God when they found themselves overwhelmed by trials and tribulation. It was the direction they looked to when they sought to have their guilt lifted from them. No wonder Jesus was so burnt up with anger when he found that this place of prayer had become an open commercial market.

In the centre of the various courts of the temple was a small enclosure that the Jews called the Most Holy Place. It was shielded from prying eyes by a heavy curtain. And there in the darkness lay the Ark of the Covenant. The ark contained the two stone tablets with the commandments which had been given to Moses.

It signified for pious Jews the very dwelling place of God on earth. It was here they believed that the glory of God was present. In the Greek version of the Jewish Scriptures and in the letter to the Hebrews the word for the lid covering the ark is *hilasterion*. It is in the same word-group that we have been considering. The King James Version of the Bible imaginatively translates it as 'mercy seat'. The temple is the place where the people are to call upon God for mercy. But it is right here at its very heart, where the glory of God dwells on the Ark of the Covenant, that we find the focal point for divine mercy.

What do we learn from this? How does it help us to understand what it means to call Jesus' death *hilasmos* for sin? We could say that God's gift of his Son to the world is the place where mercy is to be found. In the new covenant this place is not an imposing religious building on a sacred site or a holy room shielded by a curtain. It is not even the Ark of the Covenant. The place of mercy has to do rather with an event of divine and human loving which we have come to describe simply as 'the cross'. Men and women from every nation, tribe and language are invited to look towards it when they are in distress. As their trials overwhelm them, as they are weighed down with burdens too great to bear, as they are racked with guilt and self-condemnation, they are encouraged to face towards the cross. This is the place where they have been loved with a love that hurts. It is a place where mercy is to be found.

This promise of forgiveness and healing by looking to the crucifixion of Jesus is suggested in an incident that took place among the Hebrews as they journeyed across the wilderness to the land of promise. Bored with their food and angry with God for leading them out of Egypt, they complained bitterly and soon found themselves engulfed by a plague of poisonous snakes:

> . . . they bit the people and many Israelites died. The people came to Moses and said, 'We sinned when we spoke against the LORD and against you. Pray that the LORD will take the snakes away from us.' So Moses prayed for the people.
>
> The LORD said to Moses, 'Make a snake and put it up on a pole; anyone who is bitten can look at it and live.' So Moses made a bronze snake and put it up on a pole. Then when anyone was bitten by a snake and looked at the bronze snake, they lived (Num. 21:6–9).

31

In the Gospel of John this comment is made on the passage: 'Just as Moses lifted up the snake in the wilderness, so the Son of Man must be lifted up, that everyone who believes may have eternal life in him' (John 3:14,15).

The cross of Jesus, lifted high on a hill outside Jerusalem, is the place where divine mercy is to be found, a place of painful love. There is the antidote to the poison of sin. In our hour of need we can look there in hope and live!

Let us summarize what these texts indicate so far about the meaning of Jesus' death, described as *hilasmos* for sins.

It is the means by which our status before God is transformed.

It is a cry for forgiveness.

It is a place where mercy is to be found.

The Ground of Mercy

On what basis does the Lord hold back the divine sentence against penitents and grant them his mercy? The verse we have been considering indicates that it is on account of the death of Christ. His death serves as *hilasmos* for sins, the ground of divine forgiveness.

In the Old Testament, forgiveness for sin is most dramatically portrayed in the religious drama of the Day of Atonement. The central act of this annual ritual is the entry of the high priest into the Most Holy Place. Only once a year is he allowed into this sanctuary where the Ark of the Covenant lies covered with a gold 'mercy seat'. On the Day of Atonement the high priest comes into this enclosure carrying the blood of a goat which had been sacrificed outside as a sin offering. He is there, in the place of God's dwelling, to seek divine forgiveness for the sins of the people. By calling the death of Jesus *hilasmos* for sins, the writer of our verse suggests that Jesus is to be understood as such a sacrificial offering. (The Greek word used for 'atonement' is a derivative of *hilasmos*.)

But this raises all sorts of questions about God. Is God persuaded by the blood of slaughtered animals or humans to be merciful? Does he take pleasure in the killing of a man who is totally innocent? Is the spilling of blood necessary for forgiveness? To all of these, we must surely answer *no*.

The letter to the Hebrews is quite clear. The saving value of the Jewish sacrificial system is that it points forward to the day when God would freely give his own Son as an offering for sin. In themselves, the acts of religious worship and rites of the temple are but a shadow of the reality which was to come in the fullness of time:

> The law is only a shadow of the good things that are coming – not the realities themselves. For this reason it can never, by the same sacrifices repeated endlessly year after year, make perfect those who draw near to worship. Otherwise, would they not have stopped being offered? For the worshippers would have been cleansed once for all, and would no longer have felt guilty for their sins. But those sacrifices are an annual reminder of sins. It is impossible for the blood of bulls and goats to take away sins (Heb. 10:1–4).

There is no persuasive power or inherent value in animal or human blood as such or in the death of an innocent. What is it then about Jesus' death that counts with God? 'The reason my Father loves me is that I lay down my life – only to take it up again' (John 10:17).

The Father loves the fact that Jesus gave up his life freely. He loves the love his Son showed for the world. Even when they were his enemies, Jesus loved his people and gave himself up for them. Further, the Scriptures indicate it was Jesus' act of obedience to the Father in laying down his life that brought justification to so many after Adam's act of disobedience had brought widespread condemnation (Rom. 5:19). The effectiveness of Jesus' death in setting us free from guilt lies in the inherent moral goodness of his action. It was through the Holy Spirit that Jesus was empowered to live and act in this way: 'How much more, then, will the blood of Christ, who through the eternal Spirit offered himself unblemished to God, cleanse our consciences from acts that lead to death, so that we may serve the living God!' (Heb. 9:14).

What is the ground of our forgiveness? It is the death of Jesus, suffered as hilasmos for our sins; by his faith in God, his love for his enemies, his purity of life and his obedience to the Father, Jesus was able to offer himself as an acceptable sacrifice to God.

We have been looking at some verses in the New Testament regarding the love of God. They indicate that through Jesus' death being understood as *hilasmos* for sins, we who are deserving of death may come to experience eternal life.

The way this word is used in this passage suggests that Jesus' crucifixion on Golgotha can be viewed as:

a means of transforming our status before God;
a call to God to be merciful;
a place where forgiveness may be found by those who would look towards it in faith;
a sin offering which is pleasing to God because it is the loving, obedient and faithful self-offering of his own Son.

The Instrument of Forgiveness

In view of the breadth of ideas suggested by the way the word *hilasmos* is used in the Scriptures, the Good News Bible offers a remarkably helpful interpretation of the verse we are considering: 'This is what love is: it is not that we have loved God, but that he loved us and sent his Son to be the means by which our sins are forgiven' (1 John 4:10 GNB). That's it. Jesus' death is the means by which our sins are forgiven. The range of themes from the Old Testament considered above help us to conceive how that might be. But the basic idea is quite simple. Jesus' death is the instrument by which God pardons the guilty.

On 5 August 2010, after a catastrophic cave-in in the San José mine in Chile, thirty-three miners found themselves trapped nearly half a mile underground. For sixty-eight days it seemed as if the whole world was caught up in the rescue drama of these unfortunate men imprisoned together in the bowels of the earth. At great cost, using specialists from NASA and drilling experts from a number of countries, a narrow shaft was painstakingly dug through to where the miners were trapped. Once the breakthrough had been made, each miner was hoisted in a specially designed capsule to the surface to be greeted there by the joyful tears of their families and the exuberant happiness of a relieved nation.

The carefully dug shaft was the means of rescuing those miners. Being an instrument for a purpose that lay beyond itself does not mean that the shaft was unnecessary or arbitrary. It had to be dug. Jesus' death is the means by which God saves us from the consequence of our sins and grants us his pardon. It is not arbitrary or unnecessary. It had to be done. There is no way round it. If there was, then Christ died for no purpose (see Gal. 2:21). It is, however, the message of the gospel that God in his love constructed an escape route so that we might not die under the heavy burden of our wrongdoing. And that escape path is, so to speak, the death of his only Son whom he loves.

The emphasis in the New Testament account is not on God's love as a noble way of life that we are called to follow. Nor has it to do primarily with a power that overcomes evil. Rather, God's love is shown in the death of Jesus, freely suffered so that we might not perish under the Lord's righteous judgement, but live. In short, the love of God has at great cost constructed a way by which men and women may climb out of deep darkness into his glorious light.

But is it just for God to forgive men and women in this way? Or does divine justice have to be put to one side so that divine mercy might triumph?

5.

WHERE MERCY AND RIGHTEOUSNESS MEET

The death of Jesus is the means whereby God pardons men and women who have committed all sorts of crimes. Where, we might ask, is the justice in that?

This is a broader question than it first appears. The problem is that justice itself is quite a wide-ranging idea. It is not always clear exactly what we mean by it. As we consider the question about how God pardons, it might be helpful for us to think a bit more deeply about the nature of justice.

Justice has to do, at least in part, with fairness. Justice is said to be done when each person receives his or her fair share and is treated without partiality. The leaders of Israel were warned: 'Do not pervert justice; do not show partiality to the poor or favour-itism to the great, but judge your neighbour fairly' (Lev. 19:15). Such justice is an underlying feature of a realm of right relation-ships, a world of harmony or *shalom*.

The Restoration of Harmony

The importance of harmony or balance in relationships can be seen in the operation of a healthy ecosystem. All forms of life are, it would seem, subtly dependent on one another. A diverse and sustainable ecology needs to have these relationships carefully safeguarded. I grew up in a region where wild dogs were once considered to be vermin and hunted to near extermination. They were despised because of their supposed cruelty in running to exhaustion the antelope they preyed on, before tearing them to pieces. Everything has now changed. Wild or 'painted' dogs have become one of the species most highly sought after by visitors to the game parks of Southern Africa. Their particular value to the ecosystem is now widely recognized. Similarly, it was only in 1995, after a seventy-year absence, that wolves were reintroduced in Yellowstone National Park in the United States. Through their presence many believe the ecology of the park is changing for the better. With the reduction of the number of elk on which the wolves prey, two species of cottonwood trees are reviving, and, with their regrowth, erosion is being controlled and stream health is rapidly improving. The complex balance of the various forms of life suggested here is vital for ecological wellbeing.

One of the biggest threats in recent years to this delicate ecological balance was the oil spill in the Gulf of Mexico in April 2010. After an explosion on the BP drilling rig, the Deepwater Horizon, some 60,000 barrels of oil a day flowed freely into the sea, forming an oil slick with a surface area approaching 4,000 square miles. Local marine and bird life was devastated. The wildlife along hundreds of miles of shoreline was threatened. Fishing, tourism and local businesses on the coast were brought to a near standstill. The harmony underpinning the whole ecosystem had been rudely shattered. Everyone was united in the desire to achieve two goals: stopping the ongoing pollution by capping the oil leak; and clearing up the mess already made to the environment so that the ecological balance might be restored. In short, the shared goal of the community was to see things put right.

In the Bible the salvation of God is often spoken of in terms of putting right or making just. According to the Scriptures, the pollution causing the disorder that we find all around us in the environment flows out of the broken human condition. As humans are put right or made righteous, so it is believed, the creation will also be finally set free: 'that the creation itself will be liberated from its bondage to decay and brought into the glorious freedom of the children of God' (Rom. 8:21).

How does God put men and women right? The message of the Christian gospel is that he does so by forgiving them. Who has not witnessed the power of forgiveness to bring about reconciliation and restore harmony? In the New Testament the expression 'make right' or 'justify' is broadly equivalent to 'pardon'. The new 'right-eousness' that is credited to those who believe has much the same significance as 'forgiveness':

> David says the same thing when he speaks of the blessedness of the one to whom God credits righteousness apart from works:
>
> 'Blessed are those
>   whose transgressions are forgiven,
>   whose sins are covered.
> Blessed is the one
>   whose sin the Lord will never count against them' (Rom. 4:6–8).

Through the forgiveness of their sins, God brings people into a right relationship with himself. They are the special focus of his blessing. Having been put right or justified, they now experience what it means to be at peace with God. They have been brought to a place where his grace may be found: 'Therefore, since we have been justified through faith, we have peace with God through our Lord Jesus Christ, through whom we have gained access by faith into this grace in which we now stand' (Rom. 5:1,2).

We began this chapter by asking a question: Where is the justice in God's act of pardoning sinners? The answer suggested in the New Testament is that, in forgiving wrongdoers, God puts them right or makes them to be just. His act of forgiveness establishes the justice and harmony that characterizes peace. Capping a leaking oil well is a means of putting things right in a disordered environment. It is a just action in that it restores balance and harmony. So it is with the forgiveness of sin. The divine declaration of pardon is an act of justice or righteousness in that it makes men and women right before God and restores right order.

The Revelation of God's Righteousness

The Jews longed and prayed for a day of future salvation when such righteousness or justice would be made apparent in the world as God restored order and harmony to it:

Let the earth open wide,
>   let salvation spring up,
let righteousness flourish with it (Isa. 45:8b).

My righteousness draws near speedily,
>   my salvation is on the way (Isa. 51:5).

But my righteousness will last for ever,
>   my salvation through all generations (Isa. 51:8).

. . . for my salvation is close at hand
>   and my righteousness will soon be revealed (Isa. 56:1b).

Paul recognized that that day for which the Jews had looked forward to in prayerful anticipation since the time of the prophets had finally arrived through the ministry of Jesus: 'But now apart from the law the righteousness of God has been made known, to which the Law and the Prophets testify. This righteousness is given through faith in Jesus Christ to all who believe' (Rom. 3:21,22).

This righteousness of God is made known across the world in the proclamation of the gospel of Jesus Christ, the announcement that through his death our sins may be forgiven: 'For in the gospel the righteousness of God is revealed – a righteousness that is by faith from first to last, just as it is written: "The righteous will live by faith"' (Rom. 1:17).

Justice as Fair Play

Some would describe the justice or righteousness associated with bringing about right order in terms of distributive justice and restorative justice. There is, however, another sense in which justice can be understood. It has to do with determining and executing the appropriate sentence for a particular crime or in rightly rewarding noble action. It is a theme we explored briefly in the second chapter as we considered how an act of judgement, properly made, is also a revelation of truth. Now, in the light of the idea of justice as 'fair play' or 'giving to each action what it deserves', is it just for God to acquit sinners of their wrongdoings?

Paul argues that the forgiveness of our iniquities through the death of Christ is an expression of divine justice in the sense of acting fairly or justly. God's declaration of pardon to a repentant and believing wrongdoer is a disclosure of God's own essential righteousness. He is a just God: 'God presented [Christ] as a sacrifice of atonement, through faith in his blood. He did this to demonstrate his justice, because in his forbearance he had left the sins committed beforehand unpunished – he did it to demonstrate his justice at the present time, so as to be just and the one who justifies those who have faith in Jesus' (Rom. 3:25,26 NIV 1984). Paul argues that God's own justice is made known in the way he saves those who believe in his Son. Let us look at this idea more closely.

It was argued earlier that good and proper judgement is that which brings about justice. Now, the divine act of forgiveness can be considered as such a judicial decision. The truth about what the ungodly have done is brought to light in the confession of their sins and in their repentance of them. The seriousness of their transgressions is made apparent in the abandonment of God's Son to death. The sentence fits the crime. For those who are united to Christ through faith, it is appropriate that Jesus, as their near Kinsman, should stand in the dock in their stead. It is fitting that he, out of his own choice, should serve as their Redeemer, their ransom price. In God's justifying judgement of the ungodly, the process is both fair and just. In this sense justice has been served. In the forgiveness of sinners, or equivalently in the justification of the ungodly, justice is made known in the divine act of mercy.

The Foolishness of the Cross

The proclamation of Jesus' death as the means by which our sins are forgiven has been morally offensive to many over the years and continues to be so today. Some struggle with what they believe is the unfairness implicit in the idea that an innocent man should die in the place of the guilty. Some argue that God has the power and authority within himself to forgive those who have sinned against him without reference to anything else. In their view, there was no need for his Son to serve as some sort of scapegoat on our behalf. Some are appalled that violence, so evident in

40

the crucifixion, should be considered as necessary to achieve that which is good.

Paul knew what it was to have an intellectually sophisticated world pour scorn on the message of Jesus' death as God's way of salvation. But he was determined to proclaim it, for it was the means of liberating those who heard it:

> For the message of the cross is foolishness to those who are perishing, but to us who are being saved it is the power of God . . . For since in the wisdom of God the world through its wisdom did not know him, God was pleased through the foolishness of what was preached to save those who believe. Jews demand signs and Greeks look for wisdom, but we preach Christ crucified: a stumbling-block to Jews and foolishness to Gentiles, but to those whom God has called, both Jews and Greeks, Christ the power of God and the wisdom of God (1 Cor. 1:18,21–24).

Greek philosophy provided no conceptual framework within which the atonement could be understood. The idea of justice in Plato, for instance, was of no real help in understanding the corresponding themes of mercy and forgiveness. The Jews did have the concepts at hand to interpret the cross – ideas like animal sacrifice, the Passover, ransom price, redemption, the Day of Atonement, a high priest who represented the people before God. But they struggled with the obstinate historical fact that Jesus suffered an ignominious death, stapled by the Romans to a plank of wood. That the Messiah should have to suffer and die in this way at the hands of their oppressors was a stumbling block for many of them.

The persuasive power of the cross lies not in its internal logic but in its potency to change and transform lives. Those who swear by aspirin generally do so not from any scientific analysis of its composition, but from their experience of the relief it brings. Perhaps it is something like this that Paul is suggesting when he argues that the cross is 'the power of God' for those who are being saved. Through it, the crushing sense of guilt and responsibility for all of life's failures is lifted. The inexpressible peace of God is known in the turmoil of all that life throws at us. The joy and delight of worship in God's presence is tasted. The transforming power of God's Spirit energizes us in ways we could never have imagined. Here, from the world of Christian experience, are the most effective arguments for the message of Jesus' death on the cross as the basis for divine forgiveness.

Further, and as a slight to all our intellectual pretensions, the story of Jesus' death on the cross is used by God to undermine human smugness in its own wisdom and confidence in its own power:

> Where is the wise person? Where is the teacher of the law? Where is the philosopher of this age? Has not God made foolish the wisdom of the world? . . .
>
> Brothers and sisters, think of what you were when you were called. Not many of you were wise by human standards; not many were influential; not many were of noble birth. But God chose the foolish things of the world to shame the wise; God chose the weak things of the world to shame the strong. God chose the lowly things of this world and the despised things – and the things that are not – to nullify the things that are, so that no one may boast before him (1 Cor. 1:20,26–29).

In understanding the message of the death of Jesus on the cross, attitude is everything. Only the weak and the humble will be able to recognize that what happened in the garden of Gethsemane and on the rocks of Golgotha is medicine for their souls and healing for their sickness. Only they will take hold of its healing balm to be cured. And the cross will be for them *hilasmos*, the means of their forgiveness, both the place where mercy is to be found and the ground upon which it is given to them.

But further, the route by which we are made to be righteous undermines our own self-righteousness. The only way any person can ever experience true righteousness is through God's gracious act of forgiveness. We simply do not have it in ourselves, however hard we might try, to bring about our own right relation with God. Our noblest attempts to be worthy are betrayed by our faithless hearts. The sharp distinction between a righteousness that comes from our own resources and a righteousness that comes wholly from God's mercy lies at the very centre of the Christian story. To gain salvation we are to seek a righteousness that comes from outside of ourselves, freely given by God. To try and establish our own righteousness is worse than futile, for it diverts us from going to the place where salvation is to be found: 'Brothers and sisters, my heart's desire and prayer to God for the Israelites is that they may be saved. For I can testify about them that they are zealous for God, but their zeal is not based on knowledge. Since they did not know the righteousness that comes from God and sought to establish their own, they did not submit to God's righteousness' (Rom. 10:1–3).

It is not easy for a person to acknowledge that their very best falls far short of the glory of God and that the righteousness which they seek can come only as gift and never as reward. It is not easy to count our noblest achievements as mere dross so that we might discover for ourselves the righteousness that comes from God:

> What then shall we say that Abraham, our forefather according to the flesh, discovered in this matter? If, in fact, Abraham was justified by works, he had something to boast about – but not before God. What does the Scripture say? 'Abraham believed God, and it was credited to him as righteousness.'
>
> Now to the one who works, wages are not credited as a gift but as an obligation. However, to the one who does not work but trusts God who justifies the ungodly, their faith is credited as righteousness (Rom. 4:1–5).

The death of Jesus on the cross is the means by which God justifies the wicked, forgiving those who have done wrong. He is just in so doing, for through the cross he acts fairly to bring about justice or righteousness. The way of the cross displays the wisdom of God to those being saved, although in the eyes of the world it is considered as so much foolishness.

6.

THEY THOUGHT IT WAS
ALL OVER

A Ministry of Intercession

While he was dying on the cross Jesus cried out, 'It is finished' (John 19:30). Were these the words of triumph or of despair? This short sentence, spoken by a man nailed to a cross whose life was draining away, have been interpreted by many Christians to mean that Christ's saving ministry had now been completed. He had done all that was necessary for the salvation of humankind. His work was effectively over. But this is to misunderstand his mission. The free offering of his life for human sin had taken place, but there is more to the salvation of men and women than what took place in Jesus' death.

The clue to the wider ministry of Jesus is to be found in the events of the Day of Atonement outlined in the previous chapter. Slaughtering a goat and collecting its blood in a special container was only a part of the ceremonial ritual of that day. The high priest still had to carefully carry the blood of the sacrificed goat behind the curtain into the Most Holy Place. He had to present it before God at the seat of mercy. His duty there was to pray. As the spiritual representative of the people, he was to intercede with the God of Israel so that the Lord might have mercy on the guilty nation standing in silence outside. The basis of his petition for their forgiveness was the blood of the animal sacrifice in the container he was holding.

The New Testament writers recognized that this whole ceremonial drama was only a symbol or shadow of a far greater reality. It pointed forward to Jesus' own death and resurrection:

But Christ has already come as the High Priest of the good things that are already here. The tent in which he serves is greater and more perfect; it is not a tent made by human hands, that is, it is not a part of this created world. When Christ went through the tent and entered once and for all into the Most Holy Place, he did not take the blood of goats and bulls to offer as a sacrifice; rather, he took his own blood and obtained eternal salvation for us (Heb. 9:11–12 GNB).

The sanctuary that Jesus enters is not a part of this material world, a work of human hands. It is rather the very dwelling place of God: 'For Christ did not enter a sanctuary made with human hands that was only a copy of the true one; he entered heaven itself, now to appear for us in God's presence' (Heb. 9:24).

The risen and ascended Jesus now stands solemnly before the throne of the God of glory. His ministry is to represent us before the Father and to seek from him our forgiveness. This is his priestly role. He does it as one who has become man, who is like us in every way. As our representative, he must argue our cause. The basis of his argument is not that we are innocent of all wrongdoing or that our responsibility is diminished in some way and we are not really to blame for our actions. The basis of his petition is rather his own sacrificial death. Those of us who have sinned willingly, knowingly, deeply and repeatedly can still take hope: 'I am writing this to you, my children, so that you will not sin; but if anyone does sin, we have someone who pleads with the Father on our behalf – Jesus Christ, the righteous one. And Christ himself is the means by which our sins are forgiven, and not our sins only, but also the sins of everyone' (1 John 2:1,2 GNB).

Resurrection to Priestly Service

There are then two sides to the saving ministry of Christ. On the one hand, he is a sacrificial offering freely given up to God out of his unfathomable love for us. On the other, he is a high priest who intercedes with the Father on our behalf. To be an effective high priest he has to be one of us. Becoming a man has to do not just with his past life, the time when Jesus walked on earth, but also with his present existence as he now stands before

the Father. Put bluntly, there is today one who is human standing in the throne room of heaven, interceding with God for our
forgiveness.

Some find this incredible. The idea that one who is human min-
isters now in the spiritual body of a resurrected man in the presence of God pushes their conceptual boundaries to breaking point.
I recognize that this idea can be hard to get one's head around. But
it is the flip side of another amazing notion. That he who is God
lay in a Bethlehem manger, dependent on breast milk for life. The
Christian story is determined at every point by the doctrine that
the person of Jesus Christ is both truly human and truly divine.
Both perspectives need to be maintained in all their fullness without compromising each other.

Back to our theme. Jesus' death serves as an offering for our
sins. His resurrection enables him to enter as a high priest before
the Father in order to secure our justification or reconciliation with
God: 'He was delivered over to death for our sins and was raised
to life for our justification' (Rom. 4:25). Our salvation depends on
more than Jesus' death. His death has to do with him being a sacrifice for sins. His priestly role, his ministry of prayer for us, is
grounded in his resurrection. That is why the resurrection is so
important. It is not merely proof that God was with him and stood
by him. It is not simply a foretaste of the promise that we too will
one day rise from the dead. It is far more significant than that. If
Jesus had not been raised from the dead then the whole problem
of sin would not have been sorted out:

> And if Christ has not been raised, our preaching is useless and so is
> your faith. More than that, we are then found to be false witnesses
> about God, for we have testified about God that he raised Christ from
> the dead. But he did not raise him if in fact the dead are not raised. For
> if the dead are not raised, then Christ has not been raised either. And
> if Christ has not been raised, your faith is futile; you are still in your
> sins (1 Cor. 15:14–17).

It is the last few words that are so important. Without the resurrection there is no priestly ministry. The judgement against our
wrongdoing still stands. We remain dead in our sins. Our faith is
a total waste of time.

Jesus has, however, risen from the dead. And so there is hope for those of us caught up in the guilt and condemnation associated with human wrongdoing.

Confidence in the Face of Accusation

Despite our bold faces, many of us are not half as confident as we sometimes like to make out. Self-doubt and a multitude of condemning voices dog our lives. There are aspects of our inner selves that we show to very few, if any, because we are ashamed of them. Our failures leave deep furrows on our consciousness. Words of criticism haunt our memories. Sometimes these are unfounded. But they tend to hurt more when we recognize how well based they actually are. We fear the exposure of some of our less honourable deeds, for they will only bring us shame. And public shame we cannot bear. It is far easier to continue to live behind a mask and disguise key aspects of who we really are. No wonder so many of us seek therapy for our feelings of guilt.

The message of the Christian gospel to those overwhelmed by the burden of self-accusation is, however, somewhat different from the words of counsel we might receive from a secular therapist. Dietrich Bonhoeffer, the German pastor who was executed for his part in the plot against Adolf Hitler, made this penetrating observation:

> The most experienced psychologist or observer of human nature knows infinitely less of the human heart than the simplest Christian who lives beneath the Cross of Jesus. The greatest psychological insight, ability, and experience cannot grasp this one thing: what sin is. Worldly wisdom knows what distress and weakness and failure are, but it does not know the godlessness of man. And so it also does not know that man is destroyed only by his sin and can be healed only by forgiveness. Only the Christian knows this. In the presence of a psychiatrist I can only be a sick man; in the presence of a Christian brother I can dare to be a sinner. The psychiatrist must first search my heart and yet he never plumbs its ultimate depth. The Christian brother knows when I come to him: here is a sinner like myself, a godless man who wants to confess and yearns for God's forgiveness. The psychiatrist views me as if there were

no God. The brother views me as I am before the judging and merciful God in the Cross of Jesus Christ.[1]

The Christian gospel takes sin absolutely seriously. It does not diminish it or trivialize it or excuse it. The Father gave his Son for it. The Son freely gave up his life so that it might be forgiven. The matter has been properly dealt with at high cost and with great hurt. Christians are consequently encouraged to take heart when they find themselves condemned because of it:

> What, then, shall we say in response to these things? If God is for us, who can be against us? He who did not spare his own Son, but gave him up for us all – how will he not also, along with him, graciously give us all things? Who will bring any charge against those whom God has chosen? It is God who justifies. Who then is the one that condemns? No one. Christ Jesus, who died – more than that, who was raised to life – is at the right hand of God and is also interceding for us (Rom. 8:31–34).

And it is the last two lines of this passage that provide the foundation of the confidence that we might have in the face of such condemnation. It is based in the first place on the death of Christ. But there is more to it than that. It is also grounded in his resurrection whereby he is now at the right hand of God praying for us.

You might be wondering why the priestly work of Christ is being so emphasized in this chapter. But as you will see, it changes everything.

The Ongoing Work of Christ

The writer of the letter to the Hebrews offers a number of reasons why the priestly ministry of Jesus is better than the Old Testament priesthood that it replaces. One of them is that in the old system the high priests kept dying off. Again and again somebody new had to be found to do the job. The great thing about Jesus' ministry as high priest is that he lives forever: 'Now there have been many of those priests, since death prevented them from continuing in office; but because Jesus lives for ever, he has a permanent priesthood.

Therefore he is able to save completely those who come to God through him, because he always lives to intercede for them' (Heb. 7:23–25). Jesus exercises his ministry from a dimension in which there is no death. He is there 24/7 to save completely those who come to God through him. His redemptive work continues till the very end.

Jesus' ministry of salvation is not completed at the instant of his death. It is not all over the moment he gives up his spirit. What Christ has accomplished on the cross is brought into effect through his ongoing priestly service. This means that finding salvation is not limited to believing in certain truths about Christ's death. It is not primarily an intellectual relationship with a set of facts. It is, rather, an engagement with the person of the living Jesus. It is the ascended Christ at the right hand of the Father who 'became the source of eternal salvation for all who obey him' (Hebrews 5:9). Having Jesus, a human like ourselves, as our high priest is the reason we are able to enter the awesome presence of a holy God with confidence and there find mercy and grace:

> Therefore, since we have a great high priest who has ascended into heaven, Jesus the Son of God, let us hold firmly to the faith we profess. For we do not have a high priest who is unable to feel sympathy for our weaknesses, but we have one who has been tempted in every way, just as we are – yet he did not sin. Let us then approach God's throne of grace with confidence, so that we may receive mercy and find grace to help us in our time of need (Heb. 4:14–16).

The ongoing ministry of the ascended Christ changes the way we view the church and its administration.

Christ as Head of the Church

In the seventeenth century the Stuart kings of Scotland and England believed that they held their positions by divine right. They had, in their view, been appointed by God as temporal rulers of the land and as spiritual rulers of the church. The Scots, however, would not accept the idea that any man, however elevated his status, could be head of their church. That title, according to them, belonged only to Jesus Christ. A National Covenant was signed in 1638, opposing the interference of the Stuart kings in the administration of the Presbyterian Church of Scotland. The king, however, was determined to enforce his authority in spiritual matters and so it was that many Covenanters were to die as martyrs for their belief that Christ alone was Head of their church.

The New Testament describes the community of believers as the body of Christ. The gifts that the members have and the roles they play in that body are various. It is much like the variety of organs that are to be found in a human body: 'Just as a body, though one, has many parts, but all its many parts form one body, so it is with Christ . . . Now you are the body of Christ, and each one of you is a part of it' (1 Cor. 12:12,27).

Throughout the discussion on the body there is an emphasis in Paul's writing on the mutuality of the members and their dependence on one another. Their outward status might differ from the importance of the role they actually have in the functioning of the body. The important thing, however, is that they all need one another. Everyone has a vital part to play in the wellbeing of the body. The body, however, does have just one head and that is Jesus Christ: 'we will grow to become in every respect the mature body of him who is the head, that is, Christ. From him the whole body, joined and held together by every supporting ligament, grows and builds itself up in love, as each part does its work' (Eph. 4:15,16).

What a brilliant model this is for the dynamic set of relations in a Christian community! It is a radical alternative to those authority 'flow charts' which attempt to explain everything in terms of who is accountable to whom. Now here is a key question: Does Christ at present rule his church or has he left its affairs in the hands of others? To appreciate the force of this question, let me break it down into more manageable components. Does Christ continue to give gifts to the church as he himself chooses? Does he actively call men and women to various forms of ministry? Does he preside personally at the sacraments, inviting his people to share in the feast and to receive his salvation? Does he meet with two or three when they gather together in prayer? Does he continue to save those who come to him in faith? Does he send his people out into the world on the same mission that his Father sent him, filling them with his Spirit? Has he been granted all power in heaven and earth so as to lead the church to glory? In short, does Jesus Christ through his Spirit administer the life of his own church?

The answer must surely be: Yes, he does all of these things and many more through the power of his Spirit. He is the Head of his own church, personally leading it to eternal salvation. No wonder our own roles are so seldom described in terms of leadership by the New Testament writers and so often spoken of in terms of service and ministry. Through his resurrection and ascension, Jesus Christ continues to rule his church and save his people. His ministry was far from over when he died on the cross. He is still to shape and guide his church so that he might finally present her to himself as a radiant bride without stain or wrinkle (see Eph. 5:25–27).

Presenting the Christian Story

A failure to recognize the ongoing nature of Jesus' saving ministry also tends to distort the way the Christian story is presented. If everything regarding salvation has been accomplished in the death of Jesus, then the task of the preacher is simply to announce that all has already been done. The world has been reconciled to God by the death of Christ. But this is not the case. Christ is alive at the right hand of the Father to save those who come to God through him. His saving ministry is not completed but continues day and night. The death of Christ, isolated from his high priestly ministry and our coming to him in faith, saves no one.

Let me spell this out. The time of our reconciliation is not an event of past history. It might sound poetic to say the whole world was reconciled to God two thousand years ago when Jesus died on the cross. But that is certainly not the way the New Testament writers understand the matter or present it. According to Paul, he and his fellow preachers had been reconciled to God some time previously; many others were now in the process of being reconciled by God through the ministry of the gospel; but he urges his readers who are still alienated from God to be reconciled 'today' while there is still time.

All this is from God, who reconciled us to himself through Christ and gave us the ministry of reconciliation: that God was reconciling the world to himself in Christ, not counting people's sins against them. And he has committed to us the message of reconciliation. We are therefore Christ's ambassadors, as though God were making his appeal through us. We implore you on Christ's behalf: be reconciled to God (2 Cor. 5:18–20).

The message of the gospel ends with an imperative: 'be reconciled'. Salvation is the work of Christ as both sacrifice and priest. And it includes a human imperative. It is not all over. There is something for us to do.

7.

THE MYSTERY OF FAITH

We have set out on a journey in search of the heart of the Christian story. The path we have chosen to explore is the idea of the love of God as we find it in the New Testament. Whether or not this is a fruitful route can probably only be determined as we go on. Like a group of hikers, it is as we walk on that we are best able to gauge whether the track is leading anywhere. Let us continue then in the direction indicated by those first signposts, with minds that are open to the challenge of new landscapes and unexpected views.

'For God so loved the world that he gave his one and only Son, that whoever believes in him shall not perish but have eternal life' (John 3:16). The sentence takes the form of a statement of fact, but it carries within itself an implied promise. Love for the world has been costly for the Father as it has for his Son. The purpose of his immeasurable gift is that we might not suffer the judgement that is properly due to us, but rather that we might be forgiven and come to experience life eternal. The underlying promise of the text is restricted in its scope. It is for whoever believes in Jesus.

Faith as a Problem

So much is at stake in those few words. So many questions arise from them. The implications of this short phrase have perplexed Christians from the earliest times. And they are the cause of deep offence for many today. It is not easy to ignore them, for the link between the exercise of faith and the experience of salvation is not isolated to this saying. It is a theme repeatedly reaffirmed on the pages of the Scriptures:

Very truly I tell you, whoever hears my word and believes him who sent me has eternal life and will not be judged but has crossed over from death to life (John 5:24).

Jesus said to her, 'I am the resurrection and the life. The one who believes in me will live, even though they die; and whoever lives by believing in me will never die. Do you believe this?' (John 11:25,26).

All the prophets testify about him that everyone who believes in him receives forgiveness of sins through his name (Acts 10:43).

I am not ashamed of the gospel, because it is the power of God that brings salvation to everyone who believes (Rom. 1:16).

Why is the direct relation indicated here between salvation and faith so offensive to many?

First, it is for some unacceptably exclusive. What about all those who do not believe?

Second, it appears to be quite arbitrary. Why should faith be the determining characteristic of those who are to receive divine salvation? Why not love or some other human virtue?

Third, it gives the impression that salvation is ultimately dependent on us. Our believing, rather than God's loving, becomes the focus of religious attention and the decisive feature of salvation.

Fourth, it raises this perplexing question: Is faith a natural possibility for all of us or is it a miraculous gift of divine grace? If it is the latter, then where is our freedom?

These are difficult questions and they need to be addressed. In recent years, however, there has been a growing trend among Christian scholars to try and sidestep them. With the best of intentions they have sought to move the spotlight off the problematic role of faith in salvation and focus it on the grace of God in Jesus Christ. To do this some have developed the theory that Jesus not only dies for us but also believes in our place. It is argued that the expression 'faith in Jesus Christ' can often be better translated 'the faithfulness of Jesus Christ'. Others have sought to show from the Scriptures that faith plays no part in gaining salvation. It merely serves to mark out those who have become the true people of God.

There is a common thread in these and other related arguments: divine salvation does not depend on our believing. As these ideas become increasingly common, many Christians no longer think human faith is particularly significant in matters of salvation.

I sometimes have the feeling when I read these various theories that I am watching a contortionist at work. It is very impressive to see the professionalism and dedication of an athletic woman who is able to manipulate herself into a position where she can walk on her hands with her head peering out between her legs. But one comes away with the sneaky suspicion that there is something rather unnatural about it. The natural reading of the host of verses relating to faith across the New Testament is that salvation is dependent on human believing. Their consistent testimony cannot be neatly avoided by well-meaning feats of theological dexterity. It is instructive to browse through a few more of them:

This righteousness is given through faith in Jesus Christ to all who believe (Rom. 3:22).

What does the Scripture say? 'Abraham believed God, and it was credited to him as righteousness' (Rom. 4:3).

. . . if you declare with your mouth, 'Jesus is Lord,' and believe in your heart that God raised him from the dead, you will be saved (Rom. 10:9).

For since in the wisdom of God the world through its wisdom did not know him, God was pleased through the foolishness of what was preached to save those who believe (1 Cor. 1:21).

But we do not belong to those who shrink back and are destroyed, but to those who have faith and are saved (Heb. 10:39).

I wonder whether there is any other theme in the Scriptures with as much textual support as the relation between salvation and faith outlined in verses such as these. Rather than avoid the matter, let us grapple with its implications.

The Nature of Faith

'Faith' is a relative term in that its value or goodness is wholly dependent on its object. There is no virtue in believing a statement that is false or in trusting in a system that is evil. Faith can often be no more than delusion, gullibility or blind fanaticism. The virtue of Christian faith is that it has a worthy object. It believes or trusts in the person of God and the promises he makes to us in his Son Jesus Christ.

When such faith is drawn to another object, however good or noble, it becomes a perversion of itself and is no longer what it was. This means that when faith starts looking at itself and takes any confidence in its own working or delights secretly in its own ability, it becomes a sort of anti-faith, a total negation of all that it is meant to be. And so we have this paradox. Saving faith looks to and believes in God and his gracious promises in Jesus. But to place any trust in that faith is to transform it into its opposite. It is as if a couple are caught up in a passionate embrace, but the man keeps glancing into the wall-mirror to see how well he is doing. Faith is a clear and undivided focus on the one who has loved us, not on ourselves.

According to the New Testament, faith should not be considered as something that stands over against divine graciousness. Quite the reverse. Faith is the once human virtue that allows the principle of grace, God's free and generous loving, to bring about our salvation without it being muddied by our own contribution: 'Therefore, the promise comes by faith, so that it may be by grace and may be guaranteed to all Abraham's offspring – not only to those who are of the law but also to those who have the faith of Abraham. He is the father of us all' (Rom. 4:16).

God deserves all the glory for his free gift of saving love. Faith recognizes that God alone redeems us through his Son and honours him for it. That is why the promise of salvation comes by faith. Faith receives the promise as it stands. It adds nothing of its own to all that God has done. It allows salvation to be recognized as a gift and not as something that is earned. Human faith does not undermine God's grace in salvation. It is rather the divinely appointed way of honouring it.

The Model of Faith

The prime model of faith for the New Testament writers is that of
Abraham. The Jews regarded the covenant that God made with
Abraham and the promise given to him of a son as the found-
ing event of their nation. From generation to generation, parents
would tell their children how, on a clear night, somewhere in the
land of promise, God appeared in a vision to a wandering nomad
who was alone at prayer in his tent. Without children of his own,
the man despaired that he had no spiritual future and so he cried
out to God:

> And Abram said, 'You have given me no children; so a servant in my
> household will be my heir.'
> Then the word of the LORD came to him: 'This man will not be your
> heir, but a son who is your own flesh and blood will be your heir.' He
> took him outside and said, 'Look up at the sky and count the stars – if
> indeed you can count them.' Then he said to him, 'So shall your off-
> spring be.'
> Abram believed the LORD, and he credited it to him as righteous-
> ness (Gen. 15:3–6).

The story is foundational for the Jews, for it enables them to understand how they came into being as the people of God. It fulfils a
similar role for Christians. They believe that the promise to Abraham includes a reference to Christ. He is the offspring of Abraham
through whom the world will one day be blessed. As the nations
come to hear the divine promise of spiritual life and blessing and
believe it as Abraham believed, they too will be accounted righteous by God and be included among the children of Abraham.

If Abraham's faith is the model of Christian believing, what do
we learn from it of the nature of faith? Consider the following
passage:

> He is our father in the sight of God, in whom he believed – the God
> who gives life to the dead and calls into being things that were not.
> Against all hope, Abraham in hope believed and so became the
> father of many nations, just as it had been said to him, 'So shall your
> offspring be.' Without weakening in his faith, he faced the fact that

57

his body was as good as dead – since he was about a hundred years old – and that Sarah's womb was also dead. Yet he did not waver through unbelief regarding the promise of God, but was strengthened in his faith and gave glory to God, being fully persuaded that God had power to do what he had promised.

This is why 'it was credited to him as righteousness.' The words 'it was credited to him' were written not for him alone, but also for us, to whom God will credit righteousness – for us who believe in him who raised Jesus our Lord from the dead. He was delivered over to death for our sins and was raised to life for our justification (Rom. 4:17–25).

First, we learn from Abraham that faith is a response to the divine promise. Faith believes that God is trustworthy and orders its life on the basis of that trust. Faith is convinced that God has the power to bring about what he has promised.

Second, faith might begin in an instant, but it is an ongoing process. Like a clam on the keel of a ship, it clings on through rough and calm seas. Holding on becomes a way of living. While there is nothing yet visible, faith still trusts the divine promise. Abraham gave glory to God long before he saw any indication of the promise being fulfilled.

Third, faith believes that God is able to bring new life from the dead. The reason for stressing the age of the parents in the narrative of the story is to make clear that the divine promise lay totally outside of all human possibilities. God brought life out of death in Sarah's womb. He did the same sort of thing in a tomb on the outskirts of Jerusalem. Faith believes in a resurrection life that is to be experienced both now and in the future. Faith looks to God to break into our closed space-time world to resolve issues for which there can be no human solution. It grasps hold of God's promise to create life in the midst of death.

A word of caution. Expressions such as 'a commitment to Jesus', 'a decision for Christ', 'baptism in his name' have saving significance only insofar as they are indicators of a living, ongoing, wholehearted trust of God's promises in Jesus. It is through faith such as Abraham's that we are his children and so heirs of the promise of God.

The Dynamic of Salvation

Our reconciliation with God is not a static event of past history. It is not just about Jesus' death on the cross two thousand years ago. It is what happens now as we receive God's mercy through Christ, the mediator of our salvation. Christ lives to save those who approach him. His invitation to us to come to him is not a voice from the past. It is the present call of the ascended Christ to those whom he loves. He speaks to us now: 'Come to me, all you who are weary and burdened, and I will give you rest. Take my yoke upon you and learn from me, for I am gentle and humble in heart, and you will find rest for your souls. For my yoke is easy and my burden is light' (Matt. 11:28–30).

Our drawing near to him is, as it were, our act of faith. We hear the promise of salvation in the preaching of the gospel. The Spirit lifts the veil that blinds us from understanding it. The promise starts to make sense. Our hearts are softened to its offer. Our reason finds itself persuaded that truth is to be found here. We hear, we believe and we take hold of the divine promise. And in all this, the Spirit gently leads us to the risen Christ in a manner that enhances rather than undermines our humanity.

In summary, the gospel promises us peace with the Father, through the Son, in the Spirit. Salvation is a vibrant threefold interaction between the triune persons of God. It is also a dynamic event of divine giving and human receiving, of promise and belief, of invitation and response. The great Lover calls those whom he loves to the feast that he has prepared at such great cost. And the gospel proclamation charges us to receive that gift, to believe that promise and to respond to that invitation. Faith is an integral part of this gospel dynamic of salvation.

Let us look more closely at the contents of that promise of salvation.

8.

LIFE INDESCRIBABLE

There is a sense of excitement when an ancient work of art is brought up from the bottom of the sea or an object of historical significance is unearthed from one of the tombs of the pharaohs. A body of experts generally cluster round to slowly and carefully remove the layers of outer casing. There is of course frustration among observers that the process is so slow. But those who are engaged in the project know that they have to be patient. They will in due course come to the treasure within.

We have taken a few chapters to unpack the meaning of one or two key verses about the love of God in the New Testament. They lead us at last to the treasure within, to the heart of the gospel promise. It is worth the wait: 'For God so loved the world that he gave his one and only Son, that whoever believes in him shall not perish but have eternal life' (John 3:16). The promise of God for those who are deserving of judgement is that through faith in his Son they will receive eternal life – life of the age to come. It sounds amazing. What is this life eternal?

New Life Now

Eternal life is a reality that is to be experienced now. This comes as a bit of a surprise to those of us who have tended to view it only as a gift we receive when we die. But the Scriptures are quite clear that there is a present dimension to our experience of life eternal: 'Very truly I tell you, whoever hears my word and believes him who sent me has eternal life and will not be judged but has crossed over from death to life' (John 5:24). Those who believe have already moved over from death to life. It is a very powerful image. These new believers have not simply changed sides or transferred their allegiance. Their state has been radically transformed. They used to be numbered among the living dead. But they have crossed over. They are now at last truly alive. Transferring us from death to life is the purpose of God's costly love: 'But because of his great love for us, God, who is rich in mercy, made us alive with Christ even when we were dead in transgressions – it is by grace you have been saved' (Eph. 2:4,5). Salvation is about new life – new life in Sarah's womb, new life in a Jerusalem tomb, new life in the believer.

Jesus was deeply concerned that someone could be a teacher of the Jews and still not understand the necessity for the creation of new life. He said to the Pharisee, Nicodemus: 'You should not be surprised at my saying, "You must be born again." The wind blows wherever it pleases. You hear its sound, but you cannot tell where it comes from or where it is going. So it is with everyone born of the Spirit.' 'How can this be?' Nicodemus asked. 'You are Israel's teacher,' said Jesus, 'and do you not understand these things?' (John 3:7–10). The promise of salvation is the promise of life from above. It is like being born all over again. Every religious teacher should know that!

Life for Those Who Are Dead

By promising us life, the gospel indicates that those who are to receive it are in a state of spiritual death. It is a doctrine that does not flatter us. It appears rather to undermine human possibilities and natural ability, at least in spiritual matters. It certainly flies in the face of the theory that everyone has within themselves the source of salvation and needs to do no more than release the life-force within them.

In the Bible the idea of humans being spiritually dead goes back to the account of our primordial parents in the Garden of Eden and the warning given to them not to eat from one of the trees: 'And the LORD God commanded the man, "You are free to eat from any tree in the garden; but you must not eat from the tree of the knowledge of good and evil, for when you eat from it you will certainly die"' (Gen. 2:16,17).

In the Genesis narrative, the couple's act of disobedience in eating the fruit leads inevitably to their death, but it is a particular form of death. Perhaps it is similar to what happens when some relationships come to an end. The flame of desire that one of the partners has for the other is extinguished. It is not just that the heat is turned down; the pilot light in the burner is blown out. It is interesting that Adam and Eve are reported to have hidden from God when they heard him approaching. Their free and spontaneous relation with him had turned to one that was characterized by shame and guilt. They feared to be discovered in their nakedness and so they hid away from God among the bushes.

In the Scriptures, God's offer of life is made to those who are deemed to be spiritually dead, to those who are unresponsive to his love. It is God who must create the life that he promises. The necessity for the dead to be raised to life by the supernatural power of God is vividly portrayed in Ezekiel's vision of the valley of dry bones:

The hand of the LORD was upon me, and he brought me out by the Spirit of the LORD and set me in the middle of a valley; it was full of bones. He led me to and fro among them, and I saw a great many bones on the floor of the valley, bones that were very dry. He asked me, 'Son of man, can these bones live?'

I said, 'Sovereign LORD, you alone know.'

Then he said to me, 'Prophesy to these bones and say to them, "Dry bones, hear the word of the LORD! This is what the Sovereign LORD says to these bones: I will make breath enter you, and you will come to life. I will attach tendons to you and make flesh come upon you and cover you with skin; I will put breath in you, and you will come to life. Then you will know that I am the LORD."'

So I prophesied as I was commanded. And as I was prophesying, there was a noise, a rattling sound, and the bones came together, bone to bone. I looked, and tendons and flesh appeared on them and skin covered them, but there was no breath in them.

Then he said to me, 'Prophesy to the breath; prophesy, son of man, and say to it, "This is what the Sovereign LORD says: come, breath, from the four winds and breathe into these slain, that they may live."' So I prophesied as he commanded me, and breath entered them; they came to life and stood up on their feet – a vast army (Ezek. 37:1–10).

Through the word of God and the power of the Spirit, the dead are brought to life. What they cannot do of themselves God has done. He creates the life he promises.

A Different Sort of Life

This life of the age to come is quite different from all the energy, enthusiasm and vitality that some might presently experience in this world. In an engaging conversation with a lone woman fetching water at a well in the heat of the day, Jesus said, 'Everyone who drinks this water will be thirsty again, but whoever drinks the water I give them will never thirst. Indeed, the water I give them will become in them a spring of water welling up to eternal life' (John 4:13,14). Eternal life is like a spring. It seems to bubble up on its own. There is no visible means of supply. Life-giving water flows out of the ground sometimes in a rocky and dry place.

I knew Karen and Rob as an attractive young professional couple who were members in a church where I ministered twenty-six years ago. I hadn't heard from them over the years, but we made contact on Facebook a few weeks back. Karen wrote to me:

Dear Alan, it's great to hear from you. In the Lord, we are fine. Hope all is well with you, and Sheila and family. Where are you all now? Robert is totally paralyzed from advanced MS, but is still just able to swallow. I am his full-time carer. I've been coping with ME/CFS since 1997, and I have had to give up work as a solicitor. I have also just finished a course of radiotherapy for cancer, so I'm afraid I won't be much of a correspondent for a while, as the fatigue is setting in. I'll keep an eye out on Facebook though. We are missing the sort of fellowship we had in the old days, and are reliant on a Celtic Orthodox priest, who comes down occasionally from York, to bring us communion, and Christian radio for teaching. Still, as you know, this present momentary affliction is as nothing compared to the eternal weight of glory, and we are rejoicing in the Lord. God bless, Karen.

The waters of eternal life bring a level of satisfaction which is not possible to explain from outward circumstances. There is no human reason for the joy that is to be found by those who taste the life of the age to come. The Christian story has to do with the radical offer of the ascended Jesus to a world that finds itself deeply unsatisfied: 'Let anyone who is thirsty come to me and drink. Whoever believes in me, as Scripture has said, rivers of living water will flow from within them' (John 7:37,38).

Life More Abundant

There is a positive intention in the Christian story – life. The purpose of the gospel is to bring about human fullness, human well-being, human freedom. Jesus said, 'I have come that they may have life, and have it to the full' (John 10:10).

At a wedding reception Jesus turns jars of water into more wine than any joyous party of guests could possibly want. On a hillside he feeds thousands of listeners who are gathered to hear him with more food than they manage to eat. To a sinful woman he brings tears of inexpressible joy and gratitude. An unscrupulous tax collector becomes generous to a fault. Prisoners of various forms of bondage are released from their cells of addiction. The deaf hear, the blind see, the lame rise up and begin to dance with happiness. What can one say about Jesus? The gospel writer has surely got it right: 'In him was life, and that life was the light of all mankind' (John 1:4).

The Christian story rightly highlights the themes of judgement and acquittal, separation and reconciliation, sin and forgiveness. Its final intention, however, is that the offer of life might be made known and taken hold of. God loved us at great cost so that we might have life eternal.

What is this life? It has to do with Jesus.

United with Christ

It is interesting to read the apostle Paul as he struggles to find the words that will summarize the heart of the Christian story: 'the word of God in its fulness – the mystery that has been kept hidden for ages and generations, but is now disclosed to the Lord's people.

To them God has chosen to make known among the Gentiles the glorious riches of this mystery, which is Christ in you, the hope of glory' (Col. 1:25–27).

Paul argues that the message of the gospel has been hidden away from the nations for generations. Only now – as an outcome of Jesus' life, death and resurrection – is it being properly opened up. It is glorious. It is a storehouse of riches. It is the fullness of all that God has to say to us. And it can be summed up in seven words: *'Christ in you the hope of glory.'* The life of the Son is in us now, the sure expectation of the life of glory that is still to come.

The disciples of Jesus are not merely followers of his teaching or imitators of his life. The Spirit of Christ now indwells their lives. Christ is the motivator of their actions. He is the impulse of their hearts' desires. He is the wisdom that underlies their decisions. Paul was able to make the outrageous claim: 'I have been crucified with Christ and I no longer live, but Christ lives in me. The life I now live in the body, I live by faith in the Son of God, who loved me and gave himself for me' (Gal. 2:20).

The promise of the gospel is life eternal. That life is to be experienced now. It is the life of the Son of God, present in us through his Spirit. Those who believe can never view themselves in the same way again. They have been paid for, bought with a price. They belong to another. They are now temples of the Holy Spirit. They are consecrated ground, set apart for God's private use. Just like a toothbrush – dedicated for his personal use only.

Let's take a breath. We have been considering the nature of the eternal life that has been promised to those that believe. As we have seen, it has to do with Christ being in us through his Spirit. But there is a flip side to this. Eternal life is also about us being in Christ through faith. The cross-over from death to life is, as it were, an implantation into him. Wrapped up in Christ, we come to participate in all that he is:

> Or don't you know that all of us who were baptised into Christ Jesus were baptised into his death? We were therefore buried with him through baptism into death in order that, just as Christ was raised from the dead through the glory of the Father, we too may live a new life.

> For if we have been united with him in a death like his, we will certainly also be united with him in a resurrection like his (Rom. 6:3–5).

United to him by faith, we participate in Jesus' death. As he was crucified, so the dark side of our own natures is crucified. We are encouraged to recognize this and to act on it:

> In the same way, count yourselves dead to sin but alive to God in Christ Jesus. Therefore do not let sin reign in your mortal body so that you obey its evil desires. Do not offer any part of yourself to sin as an instrument of wickedness, but rather offer yourselves to God as those who have been brought from death to life; and offer every part of yourself to him as an instrument of righteousness (Rom. 6:11–13).

We share in the death Jesus died two thousand years ago on a hill outside Jerusalem. We share also in the resurrection life he now lives at the right hand of God. The Spirit that brought new life in the womb of Sarah and new life in the tomb of Jesus brings resurrection life to the new believer.

Knowing Jesus is not primarily knowledge about him. It is our experience of him. There is nothing sentimental about it. It is about suffering and pain, dying and living. Sharing in his life of love hurts: 'I want to know Christ – yes, to know the power of his resurrection and participation in his sufferings, becoming like him in his death, and so, somehow, attaining to the resurrection from the dead' (Phil. 3:10,11).

The offer of the Christian faith is eternal life. Nothing less. And this life is intimately related to our knowledge or experience of the person of Jesus: 'Now this is eternal life: that they may know you, the only true God, and Jesus Christ, whom you have sent' (John 17:3).

It is a life tasted now, but to be drunk of fully in the future glory.

Life beyond Death

The offer of the gospel is not all about life beyond death. It is about forgiveness, reconciliation, justification, peace, righteousness, joy, holiness, the Holy Spirit and life from above. And these are all to be experienced now. The focus of the gospel is on this life. Salvation is to be had in this world. Preachers are not peddlers of a product that is irrelevant to our present existence.

But the logical outcome of all these promises for those who persevere in their faith is that what they have but tasted here they will know in full measure in a life that lies beyond death. For those who faithfully continue in loving obedience, all their experience of God's grace in this world is but an entrée to the main course that is to follow. Now they sample the first-fruits from the vines; then the whole vineyard will be theirs. Now they have but a shadowy glimpse of God's glory; then they will see him face to face. Now a soft voice in their spirit whispers that they are God's children; then God himself will proclaim them openly as his rightful heirs.

The promise of the life to come, through the resurrection of the dead, is a beacon of hope for all who struggle with sickness, misfortune or persecution. They know that they will one day be set free from the shackles that hold them back, from the pain and the tears, from the suffering and the weariness: '"He will wipe every tear from their eyes. There will be no more death" or mourning or crying or pain, for the old order of things has passed away' (Rev. 21:4).

As we find ourselves caught up in suffering and trials, we are encouraged to look forward to what lies ahead, to the full measure of life eternal. This unwillingness to allow our lives to be totally determined by the misfortunes of our present reality is described in the New Testament as the Christian hope. Such an attitude of patient expectation is itself an instrument of salvation:

> Not only so, but we ourselves, who have the firstfruits of the Spirit, groan inwardly as we wait eagerly for our adoption to sonship, the redemption of our bodies. For in this hope we were saved. But hope that is seen is no hope at all. Who hopes for what they already have? But if we hope for what we do not yet have, we wait for it patiently (Rom. 8:23–25).

Earlier in this chapter I referred to a Facebook message I had received from Rob and Karen which overflowed with Christian hope. Karen's final words had been shaped by a passage from Paul's letter to the Corinthians:

Therefore we do not lose heart. Though outwardly we are wasting away, yet inwardly we are being renewed day by day. For our light and momentary troubles are achieving for us an eternal glory that far outweighs them all. So we fix our eyes not on what is seen, but on what is unseen, since what is seen is temporary, but what is unseen is eternal (2 Cor. 4:16–18).

It is as though Paul had a set of scales before him. On the one side, he heaps together all the troubles that presently beset him. On the other, he places the glory that lies ahead. In comparison to the eternal weight of glory, his suffering appears to be both light and short-lived. Like a marathon runner, he chooses to fix his attention not on his sore feet or panting lungs but on the gold medal and the future glory. Reworking the original draft of this chapter, I am aware this it is some months ago now that I received Karen's note. Since then, Rob has died and, we trust, been received by the Lord into his eternal inheritance. What is temporary has been replaced by what is eternal.

In the light of the Christian hope, it is ironic how the word 'hope' is sometimes used in ordinary discussion. A family sits waiting to hear what the doctor has to say about their desperately sick Christian mother. He emerges from her bedside and with genuine compassion says to the anxious family, 'I am so sorry but I am afraid there is no hope.' But that is precisely what there is. Hope! Hope of eternal life. Hope of glory. Hope of an inheritance that can never spoil or fade.

As always, Jesus is the model or pattern of how we should live. We are encouraged to share in his attitude: 'fixing our eyes on Jesus, the pioneer and perfecter of faith. For the joy that was set before him he endured the cross, scorning its shame, and sat down at the right hand of the throne of God' (Heb. 12:2). Looking to the joy that awaited him in the presence of his Father, Jesus was able to face up to death. And this leads us on naturally to the theme of the next chapter.

9.

FACING UP TO DEATH

The Fear of Death

Fyodor Dostoevsky, the Russian novelist, was arrested in 1849 along with a number of other members of his secret society for reading and distributing politically subversive literature. After some months in prison, he was summoned before a judge to hear that he had been sentenced to death. With only a few minutes to prepare himself, he was brought before a firing squad, his head covered with a hood. When the moment came for the final order to fire, there was a long silence. It was then dramatically announced that the Tsar had chosen to be merciful and had commuted his sentence to four years in prison. The death sentence had in fact been a hoax designed to intimidate this group of intellectual subversives and display the Tsar's clemency. But Dostoevsky was left deeply scarred by the experience. He was later to argue that the fear experienced by a condemned murderer between the time of his sentence and his actual execution was so great that the mental torment of capital punishment was actually far worse than any pain that had been inflicted on the victim during the crime.

It's not just those awaiting execution who live in such dread of approaching death. Anyone who has heard from the doctor that their cancer is malignant or that their disease is incurable knows just how paralyzing such news can be. Our fears, however, are not confined to situations where there is a sure expectation of dying. They can flourish even when death is only a vague possibility. Many find themselves worrying endlessly about the future, fearful of the sickness, accident, violence or misfortune that they sense is lying in wait for them. And, of course, they will one day be proved right. Tragedy of some sort will finally strike. It always does. To those such as these – the men and women who live in apprehension of death – the Christian gospel offers hope: 'Since the children have flesh and blood, he too shared in their humanity so that by his death he might break the power of him who holds the power of death – that is, the devil – and free those who all their lives were held in slavery by their fear of death' (Heb. 2:14,15).

Through the proclamation of Jesus' death on the cross, the gospel promises release from the fear associated with death. Life is viewed quite differently for those who have been set free by the gospel. Death no longer stands over them as an invincible tyrant. Its proud boasts are found to be hollow, its threats toothless. The grave no longer has the final say. It is not the ultimate victor in every field of combat, always triumphant in the one-sided battle with mortal humanity. No, the resurrection of Jesus has changed everything:

> When the perishable has been clothed with the imperishable, and the mortal with immortality, then the saying that is written will come true: 'Death has been swallowed up in victory.'
>
> 'Where, O death, is your victory?
>   Where, O death, is your sting?'
>
> The sting of death is sin, and the power of sin is the law. But thanks be to God! He gives us the victory through our Lord Jesus Christ (1 Cor. 15:54–57).

The sting of death is safely removed through the forgiveness of our sins. The power of sin is broken as we are adopted as children of grace and set free from the unrelenting demands of the law. In his resurrection, Jesus is like a bird in a vast aviary that has escaped through a tear in the netting. Through that same tear, all his people will one day fly free into the unrestricted world that lies beyond. In the face of death's arrogant claims and bullying ways, the Elizabethan poet John Donne gives voice to the Christ-ian hope:

> Death be not proud, though some have called thee
> Mighty and dreadful, for thou art not so,

70

For those whom thou think'st thou dost overthrow,
Die not, poor death, nor yet canst thou kill me . . .
One short sleep past, we wake eternally,
And death shall be no more; death, thou shalt die.[1]

And as death loses its power to terrorize us, so do the symptoms that accompany it, like wrinkles and grey hair, the onset of illness and the gradual erosion of strength, our loss of memory and the confusion of our minds. As we are liberated from the fear of death, so we are delivered from this whole complex of related anxieties. And in cultures such as our own, which struggle to come to terms with the prospect of ageing, this is truly good news.

Accepting the Path of Death

God demonstrated his love for the world by handing over his only Son to death. Jesus showed his love for his friends by freely offering up his life for them. He made a considered decision to go to Jerusalem, knowing that death lay in store for him there. Since Jesus was viewed as a messianic pretender and potential revolutionary by the Roman authorities, the journey to Jerusalem appeared to his disciples to be suicidal. Convinced of his divine calling to go there, Jesus believed that those who would try and divert him from it were opposing God's will in this matter:

> From that time on Jesus began to explain to his disciples that he must go to Jerusalem and suffer many things at the hands of the elders, the chief priests and the teachers of the law, and that he must be killed and on the third day be raised to life.
>
> Peter took him aside and began to rebuke him. 'Never, Lord!' he said. 'This shall never happen to you!'
>
> Jesus turned and said to Peter, 'Get behind me, Satan! You are a stumbling-block to me; you do not have in mind the concerns of God, but merely human concerns' (Matt. 16:21–23).

The fateful decision to face death when required is one that Jesus invites his disciples to make for themselves. He is not the only one

71

who has to reflect on what it means to carry his cross to a place of execution. Each of his followers must do the same:

> Then Jesus said to his disciples, 'Whoever wants to be my disciple must deny themselves and take up their cross and follow me. For whoever wants to save their life will lose it, but whoever loses their life for me will find it. What good will it be for someone to gain the whole world, yet forfeit their soul? Or what can anyone give in exchange for their soul?' (Matt. 16:24–26).

Becoming a follower of Jesus means travelling with him on a path that could lead to death. And he promises, somewhat paradoxically, that it is precisely those on that path who will discover what life really is. Those who are willing to lose their lives are the ones who will come to experience its richness most fully. They will not forfeit or lose their souls. Let us consider a little more carefully what Jesus is saying here.

We tend not to think of our souls in quite the same way people might have done a hundred years ago. But generally we still have a sense of what it means for a person to 'sell their soul'. For some it might be when an environmental activist takes a high-powered position with a giant open-mining company; for others it's when a legendary rock star and symbol of youth revolt accepts a knighthood. I first felt the force of this expression many years ago when a young friend of mine told me of his attempt to enter the Rhodesian Air Force. The officers interviewing him were concerned that as a professing Christian he might on occasion be reluctant to follow a difficult order. So they asked him whether he would obey without question the command to drop bombs on any location that his superiors specified. He was desperate to fly and recognized that his whole career depended on the answer he was about to give. With only a moment's hesitation, he assured the officers that he would do whatever he was ordered to do. The implications of his response were clear. No ethical questions would ever be raised. He would kill, without flinching, whoever they asked him to kill. I was a little older than my friend and had seen more of the 'Bush War' engulfing our country than he had. I knew that many civilian women and children were dying in the conflict and that the Air Force was not overly concerned by 'collateral damage' to the local villagers when it bombed combatants. I might have been a little naïve, but I was deeply saddened that my friend appeared to me to have signed away his integrity and so his soul without any qualms, simply so that he might become a pilot.

Since that time, I have come to understand that the temptation to sell our integrity comes before all of us in all sorts of ways. We have to face it repeatedly in the work we do and in the ventures we participate in. The pressure for us to make such a sale can be as great in the church as it is in the city. If we look back on the key decisions we have taken throughout our lives, we can usually get some idea of just how low is the price that we have placed on our souls.

Jesus calls his disciples to take up their crosses and follow him. By being willing to face death, they are no longer to be cheaply bought. They would prefer to lose the whole world with its honours and privileges, its wealth and security, and keep their integrity intact. And in that willingness they find life and discover true freedom. Jesus uses an example from the natural world to illustrate his point: 'Very truly I tell you, unless a grain of wheat falls to the ground and dies, it remains only a single seed. But if it dies, it produces many seeds. Anyone who loves their life will lose it, while anyone who hates their life in this world will keep it for eternal life' (John 12:24,25). We are reminded that as it is in the world around us, so it is in spiritual matters: life springs up out of death. This sort of dying is not always dramatic. Often it amounts to no more than a willingness to suffer a measure of personal loss or embarrassment for Christ's sake.

Consider Yourselves as Dead

To view ourselves as dead is counterintuitive. All of our senses continually tell us we are very much alive. It also appears to be a negative and limiting response to the richness of this created world to consider ourselves as dead. It suggests a harsh asceticism – the principle of self-denial for its own sake. But in the New Testament, choosing the way of the cross and being willing to lose all is never an end in itself. It is done so that life might flourish. We acknowledge ourselves to be dead in order that Christ's life might thrive in us: 'I have been crucified with Christ and I no longer live, but Christ lives in me. The life I now live in the body, I live by faith in the Son of God, who loved me and gave himself for me' (Gal. 2:20).

Believers are incorporated in Jesus' death so that his resurrection life might shape and direct the way they live. The rights of possession have been won by another: 'Do you not know that your bodies are temples of the Holy Spirit, who is in you, whom you have received from God? You are not your own; you were bought at a price. Therefore honour God with your bodies' (1 Cor. 6:19,20).

Considering yourself to be dead so that God's life might flow in you is an active, ongoing feature of Christian devotion. Imitating the worshippers at the Jewish temple, we are called to offer to the Lord not the sacrifice of a young lamb, but the sacrifice of ourselves. We hand over ownership of our lives to him. We acknowledge in ourselves the sentence of death: 'Therefore, I urge you, brothers and sisters, in view of God's mercy, to offer your bodies as a living sacrifice, holy and pleasing to God – this is your true and proper worship' (Rom. 12:1).

The purpose of the gospel is to reorientate us. Instead of all of our love being focused inwardly on ourselves, the gospel would have us live for God and for the good of our neighbours. The old way of living has to die if the new way is to come into effect. And it is the heart of the Christian message that this transformation takes place through the death of Christ. His death means our death: 'For Christ's love compels us, because we are convinced that one died for all, and therefore all died. And he died for all, that those who live should no longer live for themselves but for him who died for them and was raised again' (2 Cor. 5:14,15).

Summary

Let us bring some of these themes together. The gospel offers the believer indescribable life, the life of the age to come which is to be experienced now. The promise is, in short, 'Christ in you the hope of glory' (Col. 1:27). Through such indestructible life, the fear of death along with its accompanying symptoms is lifted. But ironically, the path that the Christian is now called to follow is the way of the cross. The cross is a symbol of hurt or cost not merely to the

Father and the Son, but also to every believer. There can be great suffering on the Christian journey. Life has repeatedly to be relinquished so that life may be found. Our bodies have to be handed back to the Father as sacrificial offerings, so that the resurrection life of Jesus might be experienced in us. Only in this way is it possible for us to become truly free – free from our fears, free to live with integrity, free for God.

The gospel is not simply about our pardon and reconciliation with God. It is about how we are now to live.

10.

THIS LIFE COUNTS

Taking the Warnings Seriously

For a few years our family owned a home bordering the winelands outside Cape Town. The veranda overlooked our tennis court with views across the sports fields to the stunning blue Drakenstein Mountains beyond. We loved the place. The neighbourhood was, however, considered to be somewhat less desirable than one might have expected from its fine outlook. This was probably because of the long-term presence in it of a number of 'bergies'. This small, resilient community form an underclass in the city's complex mix of peoples. They tend to sleep rough, drink rather heavily and generally survive both on the goodwill of the wider society and their own irrepressible humour. For generations our suburb had formed part of their traditional stomping ground. One day my young son, Courteney, heading out on his newspaper round, was startled to find a bergie had taken up residence under a large bush at our front gate along with his two dogs. Our own dog made up for his initial failure to provide proper warning by barking excessively. What were we to do with a bergie who planned to set up a temporary home in one corner of our property? After giving the matter some thought, we found a neat solution to the problem. We cut down the bush which provided his shelter. The man and his dogs moved on.

Some weeks later I found myself reading one of Jesus' parables with fresh insight:

> There was a rich man who was dressed in purple and fine linen and lived in luxury every day. At his gate was laid a beggar named

Lazarus, covered with sores and longing to eat what fell from the rich man's table. Even the dogs came and licked his sores.

The time came when the beggar died and the angels carried him to Abraham's side. The rich man also died and was buried. In Hades, where he was in torment, he looked up and saw Abraham far away, with Lazarus by his side. So he called to him, 'Father Abraham, have pity on me and send Lazarus to dip the tip of his finger in water and cool my tongue, because I am in agony in this fire.'

But Abraham replied, 'Son, remember that in your lifetime you received your good things, while Lazarus received bad things, but now he is comforted here and you are in agony. And besides all this, between us and you a great chasm has been set in place, so that those who want to go from here to you cannot, nor can anyone cross over from there to us' (Luke 16:19–26).

It did not make easy reading. The rich man allowed the beggar to stay at the gate. I moved him on. His dog licked the beggar's sores. My dog barked at him.

Now here is a question: How seriously should we take the warnings implied by Jesus in a parable like this?

Does the way we live on this earth affect what will happen to us beyond death? If we treat people badly, does it count against us at the end?

Does forgiveness mean that how we respond to others is no longer an issue for those who consider themselves to be believers?

Does receiving pardon imply that nothing will ever be held against me – that there is no need for me to have any concern about the way I have dealt with others? Will I come to glory anyway?

If we are open to hear the testimony of the Scriptures, we will soon find that there are a large number of passages that have a direct bearing on the subject. Introducing a discussion on reconciliation, Paul writes, 'For we must all appear before the judgment seat of Christ, so that each of us may receive what is due to us for the things done while in the body, whether good or bad' (2 Cor. 5:10). It would appear that our eternal reward depends on how we have conducted our lives here. It is a theme which is to be found on page after page of the New Testament. Consider a few examples from Matthew's gospel. The person who does not obey Jesus will be like someone who built their house on sand. On the day of trial they will be swept away (Matt. 7:24–27). Those who did not care practically for the brothers and sisters sent in Jesus' name will be separated out as goats from sheep (Matt. 25:31–46). If a person does not take risks by making use of the gifts given them, he or she will be thrown outside (Matt. 25:14–30). The one who does not forgive others will never receive forgiveness (Matt. 18:21–35). As for those who mistreat children, it would be better for them if they had a great stone tied around their necks and were cast into the sea (Matt. 18:6). Clergy who take pride and satisfaction in their religious status will come under severe judgement (Matt. 23:1–36). As will anyone filled with anger who verbally abuses others (Matt. 5:21,22).

The vast array of passages in the Bible on final judgement all seem to indicate that our eternal reward will be determined by the way we have lived:

> And I saw the dead, great and small, standing before the throne, and books were opened. Another book was opened, which is the book of life. The dead were judged according to what they had done as recorded in the books. The sea gave up the dead that were in it, and death and Hades gave up the dead that were in them, and each person was judged according to what they had done (Rev. 20:12,13).

The Scriptures are clear. How we live and act in this life does matter. It affects our eternal inheritance. This is a deeply disturbing notion, for it seems to undermine our future security. No wonder many have tended to avoid it. It appears to complicate the Christian story. How do we reconcile the idea of judgement on the basis of our deeds with the promise of undeserved mercy and forgiveness to those who have faith in Jesus? Before looking at how the Scriptures hold these ideas together, let us bring the problem into even sharper focus.

It Is All Over

My memory is still haunted by the ticking of a large clock in the examination room as the big hand approached the hour, signalling the end of my final mathematics paper at university. I had attempted only two of the six questions. And time was up. Our papers were about to be collected and there was nothing more I could do to influence what was bound to be a disastrous outcome.

This life counts. When we die it is over. There is no more opportunity to show kindness to the poor or love for our enemies. We cannot plant trees or feed the hungry. We are unable to affirm our children or cuddle our grandchildren. There is no longer an opportunity to apologize for the hurts we have caused or to say 'I love you' to those who are close to us. We have no time left to untangle the consequences arising from our most serious mistakes. The bell sounds, the pens are put down, the papers are collected and the project of our one short life is handed in to be assessed by the Judge of all humankind. There is nothing more we can do to influence the Examiner: 'Just as people are destined to die once, and after that to face judgment . . .' (Heb. 9:27).

One can understand why countless theories have been generated during the long history of Christianity to get around the finality of that statement. People feel they could have done better. If they could have an opportunity to explain to the Examiner what really happened, or be offered another chance to show their love and trust, then all would surely be well. But the Scriptures offer no basis for such hope. There is no indication that final judgement deals with anything other than our lives as we have lived them in this world. It is a day of assessment. The books are opened. The story is read out. The Judge has before him every thought and intention. What else needs to be said? What more can be said?

This life does count. We must take it seriously. God does. But how does this fit in with the idea of forgiveness?

Justification and Glory

A slightly overweight man is desperate to run in the London marathon. He has friends in high places and before long his admission into the marathon is secured. He soon realizes, however, that there is a world of difference between entering the race and crossing the finishing line. A great deal of training, work and perseverance is required for him to complete the course and win honour for himself.

There is a distinction made in the Scriptures between our entry into a right relationship with God and our crossing over to glory – between justification and glorification: 'And those he predestined, he also called; those he called, he also justified; those he justified, he also glorified' (Rom. 8:30). How justification and glorification relate to one another is the theme of one of our key verses on the love of God. But perhaps we should start at the beginning of the passage in which it is found to see how the argument unfolds: 'Therefore, since we have been justified through faith, we have peace with God through our Lord Jesus Christ, through whom we have gained access by faith into this grace in which we now stand. And we boast in the hope of the glory of God' (Rom. 5:1,2). Being put right by faith, we are reconciled to God and now have open access to his presence, his mercy and his grace. Yet we are also filled with hope that we will finally experience the glory of God – that we will finish the race. But what is the basis of the hope that we will get there, that on the Day of Judgement we will receive glory and not condemnation?

Paul's argument is based on the changes that are taking place in our lives. Through the process of suffering we are being transformed by the Spirit, one step at a time, to become men and women who display love to others. Of course such suffering is painful. But the fruit of it is a life that overflows with God's love: 'Not only so, but we also glory in our sufferings, because we know that suffering produces perseverance; perseverance, character; and character, hope. And hope does not put us to shame, because God's love has been poured out into our hearts through the Holy Spirit, who has been given to us' (Rom. 5:3–5).

On that day, the holy Judge of human hearts will reward the outworking of the spiritual life that he has planted in us. It is his promise from the times of the prophets that he will take hold of hard, unresponsive hearts and fashion them to be both loving and sensitive: 'I will give you a new heart and put a new spirit in you; I will remove from you your heart of stone and give you a heart of flesh' (Ezek. 36:26). He will then grant eternal life to those whom he has made great lovers of others. But we may doubt whether this will actually happen in practice. How can we be sure that the

Holy Spirit will indeed transform our lives? How do we know that his grace will do enough to save us from our own inclination to evil and so from divine judgement or the wrath of God? Paul invites us to take hope in the love of God. The argument goes like this. If while we were his opponents God gave us his Son to die for us, now that we are his children can we not trust that he loves us enough to make our lives acceptable to him through his Spirit?

> You see, at just the right time, when we were still powerless, Christ died for the ungodly. Very rarely will anyone die for a righteous person, though for a good person someone might possibly dare to die. But God demonstrates his own love for us in this: while we were still sinners, Christ died for us.
>
> Since we have now been justified by his blood, how much more shall we be saved from God's wrath through him! For if, while we were God's enemies, we were reconciled to him through the death of his Son, how much more, having been reconciled, shall we be saved through his life! (Rom. 5:6–10).

It is through God's love that we have been made right with him or justified. All the more, we can now trust that God's love will save us, making us obedient and preparing us for glory. God's love is the ground of our hope for the life to come. Jesus' self-offering and intercession procure it. Our lives, remade into the likeness of Jesus, receive it as their final reward.

We see then that our salvation has two aspects – justification and the transformation of our lives that leads to glorification. We enter the race by the pardon of our sins through the death of Jesus. We run the race with a new life that is empowered and shaped by the Spirit of the risen Christ. As with the marathon runner, there is for us some awesome work still to be done before we cross the line: 'Therefore, my dear friends, as you have always obeyed – not only in my presence, but now much more in my absence – continue to work out your salvation with fear and trembling, for it is God who works in you to will and to act in order to fulfil his good purpose' (Phil. 2:12,13).

This life counts. Or – to put it the other way round – we are held accountable for this life, for the way we run the race. Let us take that race seriously: 'let us throw off everything that hinders and the sin that so easily entangles. And let us run with perseverance the race marked out for us, fixing our eyes on Jesus, the pioneer and perfecter of faith. For the joy that was set before him endured the cross, scorning its shame, and sat down at the right hand of the throne of God' (Heb. 12:1,2).

There is much pain in the path of love, but the joy of entering the glory of God that lies ahead is inexpressible. The suffering is worthwhile. We dare not think that because we have been pardoned and made right with God, we can be complacent. We can't rest on our past experiences of salvation. We need to strive faithfully for the prize of eternal glory:

> Not that I have already obtained all this, or have already arrived at my goal, but I press on to take hold of that for which Christ Jesus took hold of me. Brothers and sisters, I do not consider myself yet to have taken hold of it. But one thing I do: forgetting what is behind and straining towards what is ahead, I press on towards the goal to win the prize for which God has called me heavenwards in Christ Jesus (Phil. 3:12–14).

Summary

All that we do during our short lives on earth has ultimate significance. The Christian hope of a life beyond death qualifies the value we might place on our material possessions and the honours we receive from our colleagues. But it highlights rather than diminishes the significance of what we have to do here – our duty to care for our planet, to love our neighbour and to walk humbly with our God.

Some Christians have downplayed the importance of caring for creation. In the light of the coming kingdom they do not recognize the significance of this material world. This I believe is a mistake, for we have been called to act as faithful stewards of the world God has given us. Others have treated holiness of life as if it was an alternative to faith. They have failed to see that faith is the proper ground for all true holiness and that a holy and obedient life is a sure indicator of genuine faith.

But perhaps one of the most serious distortions of the Christian message in modern times is the view that beyond death there is an opportunity to make amends. It is the constant theme of the biblical message that this life counts. Our world of duties pertains to this life. If there are any apologies to be made, they need to be made now. If there are certain things that we need to put right with our neighbours, then this is the time to do them. Some have in mind a speech they would like to make when they finally stand before the throne of God. Today is the day to make it. There is no place for confession or explanation when the books are finally opened and the details of our thoughts and actions are read out. It is in this world that the gospel is proclaimed. It is only here that we can be baptized for the remission of our sins, only here that we can receive mercy. We dare not trivialize our lives and actions in this world by suggesting they don't really matter, that they can all be put right later on in another place.

The Day of Judgement is a day of assessment. Hypocrisy will be shown up; truth will be revealed. Those who are not genuine will be exposed. What then are some of the characteristics of those whose faith is genuine, who will be received into glory?

11.

THE MARK OF THE BLESSED

When the lives of churchgoers are discussed, it is sad how often the question of hypocrisy arises. Those outside the faith generally have a sharp eye for the faults of those who profess faith in God. Faced with such criticisms, however, we would do well to remember that the church presents itself not as a gym for the super-fit but as a hospital into which damaged and broken people are admitted so that they might be healed. The wards of most hospitals are not overflowing with paragons of health. The beds are full of those who live in hope that they are on the mend. But are there certain symptoms which would indicate that a person is posing – that they are not genuine patients? Or conversely, is there a quality that is always present among those who have received God's pardon and are being transformed by his saving grace?

Poor in Spirit

The Sermon on the Mount is possibly the most widely honoured piece of religious literature in the world. All and sundry, including many outside the Christian church, have been heard to extol its penetrating spiritual insight. Here, it is often said, lies the heart of all true religion. It is hard to understand why this is so. Jesus' revolutionary words cut to the very heart of human pride and arrogance:

Blessed are the poor in spirit,
    for theirs is the kingdom of heaven.
Blessed are those who mourn,
    for they will be comforted.

Blessed are the meek,
> for they will inherit the earth.

Blessed are those who hunger and thirst for righteousness,
> for they will be filled.

Blessed are the merciful,
> for they will be shown mercy.

Blessed are the pure in heart,
> for they will see God.

Blessed are the peacemakers,
> for they will be called children of God.

Blessed are those who are persecuted because of righteousness,
> for theirs is the kingdom of heaven (Matt. 5:3–10).

Why should the blessings of the kingdom of God be showered on the poor in spirit, to those who mourn, to those who are meek? Why should humility be the distinguishing mark of those blessed by God?

Some people have struggled with this aspect of Christian teaching. They have described the Christian faith as a religion for slaves – one which encourages docility, subservience and suffering. It appears to have nothing good to say about the natural qualities of leadership such as a sense of superiority, dominance and self-assertion.

Why does Jesus emphasize the place of humility? And why do his words strike a resonating chord with so many? In short, why is it so appropriate that the humble should inherit the earth?

Perhaps deep down in our being we just don't like human pride and conceit in others. It seems somehow fitting or proper that the arrogant should be brought low:

Rise up, Judge of the earth;
> pay back to the proud what they deserve (Ps. 94:2).

That is why Scripture says:
> 'God opposes the proud
>> but shows favour to the humble' (Jas 4:6).

Though the LORD is on high, he looks upon the lowly,
> but the proud he knows from afar (Ps. 138:6 NIV 1984).

He mocks proud mockers
>but shows favour to the humble and oppressed (Prov. 3:34).

Love the LORD, all his faithful people!
>The LORD preserves those who are true to him,
>but the proud he pays back in full (Ps. 31:23).

Before a downfall the heart is haughty,
>but humility comes before honour (Prov. 18:12).

In contrast to human pride, there is something about the nature of a humble spirit that makes it appear as a fitting characteristic of those who believe in God's promises and receive divine grace. We would expect godliness and humility to be closely linked.

Humility and Faith

Abraham knew that both he and his wife were beyond child-bearing age. There was no natural expectation for them to have a child. They had to trust God for the promised son. Faith flourishes when there is no possibility for confidence in our own capability. Prayers are more urgent when we come to the end of our own resources. That is right and proper. The pity is that it takes us so long for us to come to that realization. Why are we so slow to ask for help? Our arrogance encourages us to believe that we have the inner strength to succeed in this life, quite apart from God. Our pride pushes us to go it alone.

A friend and I were once rescued off some cliffs overlooking the sea in North Devon. We had foolishly attempted the ascent without giving due attention to how difficult it was. Pride in one's climbing ability tends to disappear, however, when rescuers have to climb down to the ledge where you are helplessly stranded and carefully lift you off the face of a cliff. Along with profound thankfulness there is a sense of deep embarrassment. I found myself apologizing endlessly. Having to be rescued by another and being ready to place one's life in their hands tends to exclude personal boasting.

'Where, then, is boasting? It is excluded. Because of what law? The law that requires works? No, because of the "law" that requires faith . . . If, in fact, Abraham was justified by works, he had something to boast about – but not before God' (Rom. 3:27; 4:2). Faith, it would seem, is intimately related to humility. And humility views other people differently. Those who have faith in the mercy of God can no longer look down from a position of superiority on those who are outside their group. Consider again the parable of the Pharisee and the tax collector:

> Two men went up to the temple to pray, one a Pharisee and the other a tax collector. The Pharisee stood by himself and prayed: 'God, I thank you that I am not like other people – robbers, evildoers, adulterers – or even like this tax collector. I fast twice a week and give a tenth of all I get.'
>
> But the tax collector stood at a distance. He would not even look up to heaven, but beat his breast and said, 'God, have mercy on me, a sinner.'
>
> I tell you that this man, rather than the other, went home justified before God (Luke 18:10–14).

What is wrong with the Pharisee's attitude? He is at prayer, and his prayer is one of thanksgiving. He gives glory to God that his life is not in the moral mess that he sees among so many of those around him. He is a product of good spiritual habits and he is thankful to God for them. If he was acquainted with our modern idiom, he might well have looked at the tax collector and said, 'There but for the grace of God go I.'

There-but-for-the-grace-of-God-go-I religious people struggle to recognize themselves as being self-righteous or arrogant. It just seems so obvious to them that their lives have turned out much better than others'. And they thank God for it. For them it is not a question of pride. It is just a fact. As they leave their jobs in the city late in the evening and head for the comfort of the suburbs, it is inconceivable to them that the prostitute soliciting for customers outside the train station might be on the same moral plane as they are – that her sins might not be so different in God's sight from theirs. And because of that self-righteousness they will return home to their sleeping families unjustified before God.

Attributing Right Value

I grew up in a culture where success was often associated with athletic prowess. The eulogy at a funeral generally tended to include a summary of the person's sporting achievements. In many of our friends' homes there was a trophy cabinet and sometimes even a trophy room where a family's lifetime of triumphs was put out on display. Diplomas and degrees along with photographs of success might also be framed and hung on the walls. Together these mementos encouraged a sense of achievement and self-confidence. They signified that those who had won them had lived lives that were in some way worthwhile. To the next generation they were reminders of the rich sporting or cultural heritage into which they had been born.

Paul gives an account of his own heritage: 'though I myself have reasons for such confidence. If someone else thinks they have reasons to put confidence in the flesh, I have more: circumcised on the eighth day, of the people of Israel, of the tribe of Benjamin, a Hebrew of Hebrews; in regard to the law, a Pharisee; as for zeal, persecuting the church; as for righteousness based on the law, faultless' (Phil. 3:4–6). He comes from a noble lineage and a proud tradition. The emphasis is on religion rather than sport, academia or culture. His background nevertheless serves as the ground for his self-confidence. But to be justified before God, Paul had to learn how to attribute proper value to this rich heritage: 'But whatever were gains to me I now consider loss for the sake of Christ. What is more, I consider everything a loss because of the surpassing worth of knowing Christ Jesus my Lord, for whose sake I have lost all things. I consider them garbage, that I may gain Christ' (Phil. 3:7,8).

So that he might be found in Christ, having a righteousness that comes from God, Paul considered all the fine things about his heritage as just so much garbage. It is a comparative estimate. As a king might forgo his crown, considering it to be worthless, in order that he could marry the woman he loves, so Paul views his religious heritage.

Humility means placing low value on all our greatest achievements, our culture, our heritage, our race and our nationality so that we might take hold of the treasure of true worth.

The kingdom of heaven is like treasure hidden in a field. When a man found it, he hid it again, and then in his joy went and sold all he had and bought that field.

Again, the kingdom of heaven is like a merchant looking for fine pearls. When he found one of great value, he went away and sold everything he had and bought it (Matt. 13:44–46).

Humility does not mean having no pride at all. It is rather about having pride in the right things. It is about a confidence that is well placed:

Therefore, as it is written: 'Let the one who boasts boast in the Lord' (1 Cor. 1:31).

May I never boast except in the cross of our Lord Jesus Christ, through which the world has been crucified to me, and I to the world (Gal. 6:14).

This raises further questions: How confident should a person be in their eternal destiny? How does such confidence tie in with humility?

The Fear of the Lord

The Song of Mary is another one of those pivotal passages of Scripture with a radical message that has surprisingly achieved widespread popularity. Consider the following section:

His mercy extends to those who fear him,
    from generation to generation.
He has performed mighty deeds with his arm;
    he has scattered those who are proud in their inmost thoughts.
He has brought down rulers from their thrones
    but has lifted up the humble.
He has filled the hungry with good things
    but has sent the rich away empty (Luke 1:50–53).

The kingdom of heaven brings about a dramatic turning of tables. The proud are scattered; the humble are lifted up. Of particular significance for our discussion is the expression 'His mercy extends to those who fear him.' What does it mean to fear the Lord? The phrase is commonly used throughout the Bible simply as a way of identifying those who are worshippers of God. The context, how- ever, sometimes gives clues as to its more precise meaning. Con- sider its use in a psalm we looked at earlier:

If you, O LORD, kept a record of sins,
O Lord, who could stand?
But with you there is forgiveness;
therefore you are feared (Ps. 130:3,4 NIV 1984).

Forgiveness brings about the fear of the Lord. This would suggest that fearing God has to do with either thankfulness or worship or perhaps even commitment to him.

On a number of occasions the context indicates that the fear of God is related to an appreciation of his divine power or a recognition of his role as our final Judge.

He did this so that all the peoples of the earth might know that the hand of the LORD is powerful and so that you might always fear the LORD your God (Josh. 4:24).

For we must all appear before the judgment seat of Christ, that each of us may receive what is due to us for the things done while in the body, whether good or bad.
Since, then, we know what it is to fear the Lord, we try to per- suade others (2 Cor. 5:10,11).

I tell you, my friends, do not be afraid of those who kill the body and after that can do no more. But I will show you whom you should fear: Fear him who, after your body has been killed, has au- thority to throw you into hell. Yes, I tell you, fear him (Luke 12:4,5).

Here the fear of the Lord is associated with a sense of awe in his power or a respect for his role as Judge of all humankind. This would suggest that the fear of God is a positive response to his ultimate authority over us, to his immeasurable power and to his awesome holiness. It is a powerful motivation for personal sanctification and obedient service.

Now if God's mercy is for those who fear him, we have this paradox. God works graciously in the lives of those who are filled with awe by the prospect of standing before him in judgement. But such an attitude is ironically an indicator that they have nothing to fear from that day of reckoning.

However, those who do not fear God, who are not humbled by his authority, his holiness or the expectation of his judgement, are set apart from his mercy. There are good reasons for them to be concerned on that day.

Summary

Let us bring together some of our recent themes. Humility in the awesome presence of God and before our neighbours is a sure mark of divine graciousness in the life of a believer. It is the natural outworking of true faith in God. It is also the fertile soil in which a genuine faith flourishes. Linking up with some of the ideas of the last chapter, we might say that God calls his people to seek justice for those who are treated unfairly, to act with kindness to all who have suffered loss and to live before him and our neighbours in humility:

> He has shown you, O mortal, what is good.
>> And what does the LORD require of you?
> To act justly and to love mercy
>> and to walk humbly with your God (Mic. 6:8).

12.

MAKING THE FIRST MOVE

We have been on a search for the heart of the Christian story. Journeying through the Bible's rich and diverse world of ideas and stories, we have been following a route marked out by one particular theme – the love of God. The meaning of this idea as it is explained in three key verses in the New Testament has determined the path on which we now find ourselves. Our exploration has led us to consider the costliness of that love, the judgement from which it saves us, the sort of life which it promises and the role that faith plays in responding to it. The saving ministry of Jesus has been considered afresh in the light of it. We have also reflected on why these short lives of ours have ultimate significance and what is the distinguishing mark of those who are truly blessed by God. It is as though we had decided to tour historic London from an excursion cruiser on the river Thames. Of course we are bound to miss much of the suburban scenery from the deck of the motor launch. But the city's long history has been so bound up with the river that many of its most famous landmarks are likely to come into view at some stage on our journey. Likewise the love of God is so closely bound to the theme of salvation that the one will inevitably shed light on the most significant features of the other.

He First Loved Us

As we continue our exploration of the theme of God's love, it is apparent that there is an important dimension of that love which we have not yet considered. It has to do with the pre-emptive role that divine love plays in bringing us back to God. 'This is love: not that we loved God, but that he loved us and sent his Son as an atoning sacrifice for our sins' (1 John 4:10).

My wife Sheila and I once went on a marriage course led by my youngest brother and his wife. A number of couples from our congregation duly met up at our home for dinner and an introductory session before the course began. We started with what was meant to be a light, ice-breaking exercise. Each partner was asked who had initiated their relationship. I could hardly believe the high drama that followed. Some of the women were deeply offended by the suggestion that they had played a leading role in their courtship. One of the men found it extremely unhelpful when his wife disclosed how she had already had plans for the wedding before their relationship had even got off the ground. It took twenty minutes to restore some sort of calm to our lounge. So much for light entertainment!

It can be quite humbling for a person of faith to look back and learn that their free response to the promise of salvation was part of some greater divine purpose – that God had planned the outcome of their relationship before they had even warmed up to the idea. They struggle with the thought that he chose them long before they had decided for him. Such an idea appears to undermine their personal sense of freedom. Yet it is an integral aspect of the Christian story that God's love does come first. He initiates the relationship with us. It is he who seeks us out. Francis Thompson lay destitute and forsaken at Charing Cross Station when he wrote his poem, 'The Hound of Heaven':

> I fled Him, down the nights and down the days;
> I fled Him, down the arches of the years;
> I fled Him, down the labyrinthine ways
> Of my own mind; and in the midst of tears
> I hid from Him, and under running laughter.
>   Up vistaed hopes I sped;
>   And shot, precipitated,
> Adown Titanic glooms of chasmed fears,
> From those strong Feet that followed, followed after.
>   But with unhurrying chase,
>   And unperturbèd pace,

Deliberate speed, majestic instancy,
>   They beat – and a Voice beat
>   More instant than the Feet –
'All things betray thee, who betrayest Me.'[1]

The Christian story is a romance describing how God in his love pursued us while we were running away from him. He came to our aid while we were too weak to help ourselves. He loved us while we were still his enemies. 'You see, at just the right time, when we were still powerless, Christ died for the ungodly. Very rarely will anyone die for a righteous person, though for a good person someone might possibly dare to die. But God demonstrates his own love for us in this: while we were still sinners, Christ died for us' (Rom. 5:6–8).

What is the value of this idea that it was God who first loved us – that he chose to be our God before we chose to be his people? Well, for those of us who have been disloyal to him, and who are deeply aware of the continuing flaws in our characters, it is a source of great encouragement to know that we were the object of his desire before our relationship even started. Of course a doctrine of divine election can be misused and has sometimes been the occasion for sectarian self-righteousness and arrogant conceit. But its proper purpose is surely to humble our human hearts so that we might look to God's abounding graciousness rather than to our own inadequate responses as the ground of our salvation. It is in him and not in us that we find a sure foundation for our future hope. What he began in us, he will bring to completion. 'For we are God's handiwork, created in Christ Jesus to do good works, which God prepared in advance for us to do' (Eph. 2:10).

But doesn't this emphasis on the priority of God's love in winning us to himself and in shaping our lives undermine our free will? What does it mean to be his workmanship?

Divine Purpose and Human Willing

Sophie's World is a very cleverly written novel, full of all sorts of intellectually challenging ideas.[2] At one stage in the book the characters have a discussion about their own freedom of choice. They are clearly exercising that freedom as they debate a number of deep and important questions that are troubling them. They certainly don't appear to be under any external constraints. But then they ask one another whether they are actually free from the author's intention – from the plot of the book in which they are the principal characters. It would seem to the reader that they have their freedom, but it is always a freedom that lies within the author's grand design. We might say that good writers of fiction respect the freedom of their characters but nevertheless use it to construct the plot that they, the author, have in mind.

This illustration, although inadequate in many respects, can nevertheless open us to the possibility that humans are able to exercise their freedom within God's purpose. A Christian doctrine of creation requires that creatures have a genuine creaturely liberty to be themselves, to act in conformity with their own characters and respond with integrity to their surroundings. It means that humans are responsible not merely for the decisions that they make but for the habits and personalities which are formed by those decisions. Nevertheless, although they each have their own integrity and remain personally accountable for their actions, they are at the end of the day still only creatures, totally dependent on their Creator for every breath they take, for every electronic impulse that enables their thoughts.

Further, there are all sorts of ways in which we are not half as free as we would like to think. The alcoholic man in the pub can choose whatever beverage he likes, but how free is he not to take a drink? How free are those who have enjoyed power to relinquish it gracefully? How free is the materialist to forgo their great wealth? What freedom does the one consumed by bitterness have to forgive? How free are those who are aware of their advancing years to put aside their nagging fear of age and death? Are the proud genuinely free to be humble? Are liars free to own up to the web of deceit that they have spun for themselves and come clean at last? Is the sexually immoral person free to live in purity? No, in these various ways and perhaps others, we have all, it seems, become slaves to our own dark habits and practices.

As it is in the world of morality, so it is in spiritual matters. Are the self-righteous quite free to call out to God for mercy? Are self-made men and women able to trust in God for their salvation?

Can the cynical believe in the divine promises? Are those who are totally absorbed in their own lives able to love God with all their heart, soul, mind and strength?

Helpless in Ourselves

The Scriptures indicate that divine love must initiate our reconciliation with God, for we no longer have the capacity within ourselves to do it. The veil that blinds our vision must be lifted up so that we can see. Like Lazarus, the spiritually dead must be called to life so that they might be filled with the light of Christ:

> Wake up, sleeper,
>   rise from the dead,
>   and Christ will shine on you (Eph. 5:14).

We hear the promise of salvation and we respond to it in faith, running joyfully to the person of Christ. But on later reflection we come to recognize that the initiative was not ours but his. We ran speedily because we were being drawn as if by a powerful magnet towards the one lifted high on the cross:

> And I, when I am lifted up from the earth, will draw all people to myself (John 12:32).

> No one can come to me unless the Father who sent me draws them, and I will raise them up at the last day (John 6:44).

God's initiating love came upon us while we were spiritually without life, trapped in a world of self-deceit, serving dark unknown forces and deserving of his divine judgement:

> As for you, you were dead in your transgressions and sins, in which you used to live when you followed the ways of this world and of the ruler of the kingdom of the air, the spirit who is now at work in those who are disobedient. All of us also lived among them at one time, gratifying the cravings of our flesh and following its desires and thoughts. Like the rest, we were by nature deserving of wrath. But

because of his great love for us, God, who is rich in mercy, made us alive with Christ even when we were dead in transgressions – it is by grace you have been saved (Eph. 2:1–5).

One implication of this pre-emptive love is that those who experience God's grace have no reason for arrogance, no grounds for boasting. There remains in them the possibility for humility, the basis of Christian spirituality: 'For it is by grace you have been saved, through faith – and this not from yourselves, it is the gift of God – not by works, so that no one can boast' (Eph. 2:8,9).

It was the theme of the previous chapter that God blesses the humble. But the converse is equally true. Those who have been blessed by God's initiating grace are truly humbled. There is absolutely no reason for any arrogance on their part.

Those who have fallen deeply in love find themselves amazed in two quite different ways. First, they are taken up with the sheer excellence of the one on whom their love has fallen. But second, and more profoundly, they find it incredible that a person with such virtues should actually be in love with them. This is truly humbling.

Difficulties with the Doctrine

Let us return to our theme. Why, we might ask, has a doctrine of the pre-emptive love of God proved to be so difficult for many? Some Christians are concerned that any emphasis on the priority of divine action can be morally paralyzing for those who are yet to be captivated by the story of the cross. For what can a person possibly do whose eyes have not been opened to the truth of the gospel, whose heart is still untouched by the costly love of the Father? How does it help them to hear that God must act first? Surely the theme of the initiating love of God should be a matter for mature reflection, a word of encouragement for those looking back on their journey of faith. Surely, it can't be an integral part of the good news as it is presented to an unbelieving world.

I have some sympathy with such concerns. The gospel, as we have seen earlier, does call for a response among those who hear it. And the hearers of its message are accountable for the response they give to it. Nowhere in the New Testament is anyone encouraged to wait a while until God softens their heart or opens their eyes so that they might be able to call on the name of the Lord. No preparation needs to be made prior to repenting and believing in the gospel. As we shall see in the final chapter, the Christian proclamation takes the form of divine promise. And those who hear that promise are challenged to take hold of it and rejoice in it without delay.

And yet our responsibility to respond to the divine promise in faith and to strive for eternal salvation is repeatedly offset in the Scriptures by the doctrine that it is God who enables us to do what he requires of us. Even in fulfilling our duty we are to trust in his gracious action: 'Therefore, my dear friends, as you have always obeyed – not only in my presence, but now much more in my absence – continue to work out your salvation with fear and trembling, for it is God who works in you to will and to act in order to fulfil his good purpose' (Phil. 2:12,13).

Further, there are times when a clear emphasis on the divine initiative in salvation can be a powerful encouragement for faith and a stimulus for prayer among those of us caught up in the battle with sin and the reality of evil. Sometimes poetry can express these matters of deep spiritual paradox more adequately than prose. Consider this seventeenth-century sonnet by the preacher John Donne. Its language and style are likely to be somewhat strange to a modern ear and it might be of help to read it more than once:

Batter my heart, three-personed God; for, you
As yet but knock, breathe, shine, and seek to mend;
That I may rise, and stand, o'erthrow me, and bend
Your force, to break, blow, burn, and make me new.
I, like an usurped town, to another due,
Labour to admit you, but oh, to no end,
Reason, your viceroy in me, me should defend,
But is captived, and proves weak or untrue,
Yet dearly I love you, and would be loved fain,
But am betrothed unto your enemy,
Divorce me, untie, or break that knot again,
Take me to you, imprison me, for I,

98

Except you enthral me, never shall be free,
Nor ever chaste, except you ravish me.[3]

Summary

God loved us before we loved him. God's love is pre-emptive. It seeks us out long before we start looking for him. We are discovered by it and drawn willingly towards it. We exercise our creaturely freedom, responding to divine grace, believing his promise and following his way without any coercion or compulsion. And yet such freedom is always practised within the hospitality of the divine purpose. God's will will be done.

We turn, finally, to consider the nature of the divine offer of salvation.

13.

THE PROMISE AS GIFT

What form does the Christian story of good news take? Is it a narrative of events – the account of a man from above who lived among us, died and rose again? Is it a pattern of spirituality – a presentation of how, through his life, we ourselves are to live? Or is it in essence no more than a promise, a divine pledge that is to be grasped firmly by faith? The argument of this final chapter is that the gospel is such a promise and that in that promise all else is included. Everything that is for our good, whether on earth or in heaven, in the present or in the future, is bound up in the divine offer that lies at the heart of the gospel.

The Son as Gift

Our reflections on the love of God have suggested that the Christian story takes the form of an implied promise. Let us return to one of our three foundational texts: 'For God so loved the world that he gave his one and only Son, that whoever believes in him shall not perish but have eternal life' (John 3:16).

In the first chapter, our focus as we explored this passage was on the demonstration of God's costly love for the world in handing his Son over to death. In this chapter the emphasis will shift slightly. It will highlight the gift of God's Son as the Father's gift to us. In short, the pledge of the gospel is identified with the gift of Jesus: 'He who did not spare his own Son, but gave him up for us all – how will he not also, along with him, graciously give us all things?' (Rom. 8:32).

One weekend, while our younger son was away from home studying, my wife and I drove out of London to visit him in his university digs. One of his flatmates was a young Christian who was in the habit of sticking scraps of paper all over the walls with his favourite biblical verses written on them. The place had become untidy, and a team decision was duly made that texts could be posted by the new convert only in his own bedroom and in the toilet. I don't know what his bedroom looked like but the toilet was a sight to behold. There was almost no free space left. As one sat down, one could read promises that applied to almost every conceivable situation one might face. There was hope for the downcast, strength for those being tempted, life for those who believe. Families and friends were promised to those who gave up all to follow Jesus. Freedom was offered to all who held on to his teaching. The loyalty of Jesus before the judgement seat of God was pledged to whoever was loyal to him now. I can't remember the details but it seemed then that all the treasures that heaven could offer were right there for the taking. What holds together such a glorious array of divine promises? 'For no matter how many promises God has made, they are "Yes" in Christ' (2 Cor. 1:20).

All of the Father's promises find their fulfilment in Jesus. His life, death, resurrection and intercession are the ground of all the blessings that we are to receive from God. He is the great storehouse where, if we would but realize it, all the treasures of God are to be found. Paul's hope is that his hearers 'may have the full riches of complete understanding, in order that they may know the mystery of God, namely, Christ, in whom are hidden all the treasures of wisdom and knowledge' (Col. 2:2,3).

The promise of Christ is a central theme of the Scriptures. The two disciples on the Emmaus road were slow to understand this, and Jesus had to help them: 'And beginning with Moses and all the Prophets, he explained to them what was said in all the Scriptures concerning himself' (Luke 24:27). The promise of Jesus was foreshadowed in various aspects of Jewish worship such as the Passover lamb, the Levitical priesthood and the blood of sacrificial animals. It was suggested in the great stories of national deliverance that parents passed on to their children – the manna that came down from heaven, the water that flowed from the rock in the desert, Jonah's rescue by the great fish, and the bronze serpent of healing that was raised up high among the dying Hebrews. To a nation dominated by foreign powers, the promise took vivid shape in the pledge of a future Messiah,

the anointed Davidic king, who would bring about the coming kingdom of God. It was a promise that gave to a dispirited and scattered
people hope that one day God would liberate them from foreign rule
and govern them through a divinely appointed king:

> For to us a child is born,
>> to us a son is given,
>> and the government will be on his shoulders.
> And he will be called
>> Wonderful Counsellor, Mighty God,
>> Everlasting Father, Prince of Peace.
> Of the greatness of his government and peace
>> there will be no end.
> He will reign on David's throne
>> and over his kingdom,
> establishing and upholding it
>> with justice and righteousness
>> from that time on and for ever.
> The zeal of the LORD Almighty
>> will accomplish this (Isa. 9:6,7).

Occasionally, the promise had a more tragic tone and portrayed
the one to come as a suffering servant. It was a perspective
which later generations would find particularly difficult to
buy into. They could not conceive why the promised Messiah
should have to suffer; why God's love should prove to be so
costly; why it could not be demonstrated in the exercise of brute
power:

> Surely he took up our pain
>> and bore our suffering,
> yet we considered him punished by God,
>> stricken by him, and afflicted.
> But he was pierced for our transgressions,
>> he was crushed for our iniquities;
> the punishment that brought us peace was on him,
>> and by his wounds we are healed.
> We all, like sheep, have gone astray,
>> each of us has turned to our own way;

and the LORD has laid on him
>the iniquity of us all (Isa. 53:4–6).

An old man named Simeon had waited all his life for God to fulfil these promises. The Spirit had disclosed to him that he would not die until he had seen the Messiah with his own eyes. One day, two young parents brought their baby to the temple to be blessed. Simeon took the child Jesus in his arms and praised God, saying:

Sovereign Lord, as you have promised,
>you may now dismiss your servant in peace.
For my eyes have seen your salvation,
>which you have prepared in the sight of all nations:
a light for revelation to the Gentiles,
>and the glory of your people Israel (Luke 2:29–32).

The promise of Jesus as God's gift to the world had finally appeared. To receive the Father's promise is, in the language of faith, to take firm hold of his Son, knowing that in him is both pardon and life eternal.

The Spirit as Gift

Alongside the Father's gift of the Son, and dependent on it, is a second divine pledge – the Father's gift of the Spirit to us. When Jesus was about to leave this world, he explained to his disciples that a second promise remained: 'Do not leave Jerusalem, but wait for the gift my Father promised, which you have heard me speak about. For John baptised with water, but in a few days you will be baptised with the Holy Spirit' (Acts 1:4,5). And so we find that flowing together with the promise of the Messiah in the Scriptures there is a second stream of hope – the promise of the Holy Spirit. What had been known in special circumstances for acts of particular service and among relatively few would in the last days be the common experience of multitudes. The promise of the Spirit announced by the prophet Joel was recognized by Peter as being fulfilled on the Day of Pentecost:

In the last days, God says,
> I will pour out my Spirit on all people.
Your sons and daughters will prophesy,
> your young men will see visions,
> your old men will dream dreams (Acts 2:17).

Having ascended to the presence of the Father, Jesus was able to give the Spirit to his disciples: 'Exalted to the right hand of God, he has received from the Father the promised Holy Spirit and has poured out what you now see and hear' (Acts 2:33).

How are we to understand the relation between the gift of the Spirit and the gift of the Son?

In front of the British parliament is a statue of England's legendary king, Richard the Lionheart. He is mounted and in full battle-dress with his sword raised. Returning from a long campaign, Richard was shipwrecked on the Italian coast and had to travel through hostile European territory disguised as a low-ranking pilgrim. He was recognized and taken prisoner near Vienna. The local sovereign was a man he had once humiliated. For his release, a ransom of some 65,000 pounds of silver was demanded from the English people, more than twice the country's annual tax revenue. While Richard languished as a captive in Dürnstein Castle he wrote this song, here translated by Henry Adams from the French:

> No prisoner can tell his honest thought
> Unless he speaks as one who suffers wrong;
> But for his comfort he may make a song.
> My friends are many, but their gifts are naught.
> Shame will be theirs, if, for my ransom, here
> I lie another year.[1]

The king's ransom was eventually raised at great cost to the people of England. A large part of it also came from the gold and silver ceremonial vessels of the churches. The full amount having been collected, there was a natural concern that the treasure chests might be waylaid on their route to Germany. They were eventually transported across Europe and delivered intact to those who held him captive by the ambassadors of the

Holy Roman Emperor. On 4 February 1194, the ransom having been paid in full, Richard the Lionheart was set at liberty.

Those with an eye of faith might recognize in this story a parable of their own plight. They are the once proud prisoner, now held captive in a foreign fortress, chained up in their fears by powerful forces, suffering the consequences of their past arrogance. It is they who write sad songs of inexpressible longing, calling out for deliverance. Jesus remains for them the one true Friend in time of need, whose suffering and death purchase a ransom price, the value of which is more than enough to set them and a world of other prisoners free. But it is the Holy Spirit who carries that treasure chest, collected at such great cost, to the very dungeon in which they are being held, so that the prison doors may swing open. It is the Spirit who opens their ears so that they might hear news of such deliverance, who gives sight to their eyes so that they might believe in the value of such a ransom and who empowers their feeble legs so that they might walk free from the prison and head for home.

In short, the Holy Spirit carries all that Jesus has achieved and applies it to the life of the believer: 'He will glorify me because it is from me that he will receive what he will make known to you. All that belongs to the Father is mine. That is why I said the Spirit will receive from me what he will make known to you' (John 16:14,15). It is the Spirit who takes our hearts of stone and makes of them soft hearts, sensitive to the world around us. It is the Spirit who writes God's law on those hearts so that we might learn to love and enjoy that which is truly good. It is through the Spirit that we come to recognize, deep in our beings, that we are God's children, and it is by the Spirit that we are enabled to mumble back to God the prayers that flow from his own heart. It is by the Spirit that our dark deeds are put to death. Slowly, step by step, the Holy Spirit transforms our flawed lives into the likeness of Jesus so that one day we shall be like him.

There are then two sides to the offer of the gospel. The Father gives his Son for us to purchase for us both forgiveness and life eternal. He gives his Spirit to us so that all that Jesus has done, and continues to do on our behalf, might bear fruit in our lives.

The River of Blessing

These two streams of divine blessing – the gift of the Son and the gift of the Holy Spirit – flow from a single source. They are, we might say, two branches of one great river.

This one vast river of promise is made explicit almost every time God enters into agreement or covenant with his people. It is the overarching feature of all that he will bless them with. It is the summary of his great gift to us. It is the fullness of the gospel:

I will walk among you and be your God, and you will be my people (Lev. 26:12).

'This is the covenant that I will make with the people of Israel
    after that time,' declares the LORD.
'I will put my law in their minds
    and write it on their hearts.
I will be their God,
    and they will be my people' (Jer. 31:33).

I will give them a heart to know me, that I am the LORD. They will be my people, and I will be their God, for they will return to me with all their heart (Jer. 24:7).

Then you will live in the land I gave your ancestors; you will be my people, and I will be your God (Ezek. 36:28).

And I heard a loud voice from the throne saying, 'Look! God's dwelling-place is now among the people, and he will dwell with them. They will be his people, and God himself will be with them and be their God' (Rev. 21:3).

The triune God promises that he himself will be our God, even as we shall be his people. He promises that he will be our protection and our strong tower. He will love us with an everlasting love. He will be faithful towards us in time and in eternity. He will overwhelm the forces of darkness that stand up against us. He will satisfy us with every good thing. And when we pass through the valley of the shadow of death, he will be with us.

The promise of the gospel can be summarized in words such as these. God in love gives himself to us. He does so through two acts of infinite generosity – the gift of his Son on our behalf and the gift of his Spirit to us.

Summary

Jesus was in conversation with a Samaritan woman who was deeply unsatisfied with the way her life was turning out. He said to her, 'If you knew the gift of God and who it is that asks you for a drink, you would have asked him and he would have given you living water' (John 4:10). There is a disarming simplicity about the gospel. Those who have recognized the gift of God will surely ask his Son for it. And he will give to them the water of life.

This life is purchased by the death of Jesus and procured by his prayers at the Father's right hand. It is applied to our lives by the Spirit of Jesus, opening our eyes to see his glory and our hearts to know his love. He gives strength to us who are weak so that we might serve him faithfully. In short, we come by Jesus, through the Spirit, to God the Father who promises to be our God even as we are made to be his people.

14.

DEBRIEFING

The Gospel

This book has the outward form of a travel guide. It has suggested a route that might be taken by anyone who would like to investigate for themselves the heart of the Christian story. The signposts indicating the path are a group of texts on the love of God in the New Testament. Led by them, we have found ourselves exploring a whole range of connected themes in the Scriptures. It has not been a journey for the faint-hearted. For those with their eyes open, the views have sometimes been exhilarating, sometimes awe-inspiring, sometimes deeply humbling, and sometimes they have challenged us to the core of our being. Now that the trip is over, we ought to take stock and ask what it is that we have found. What can we say about the gospel story?

At its heart there is a remarkable simplicity about the Christian story. The triune God in costly love offers himself to be our God. There are two movements in this act of divine self-offering, the second flowing out of the first. On the one hand the Father gives up his only Son for our sins so that we might be put right with him. On the other, he gives his Spirit to us so that we might be made holy, bearing his likeness. His promise is that in Christ we may have eternal life, life of the age to come. This life is to be enjoyed now in the world of our present existence. It is new, vital and totally transforming, like being born all over again. But eternal life is also life beyond death. It is the full measure of what can only be sampled now.

Our new life here has ultimate significance. We are to act justly, to love mercy and to walk humbly with our God. It is our calling to make known his mighty acts of salvation and to serve as living witnesses to the glory of his character. How our faith is worked out in practice will be the basis for the final judgement that is to be made on our lives. But it is a judgement we need not fear. For in his ongoing ministry at the Father's right hand, Christ stands up for us and defends us. By his Spirit he renews us, keeping us safe and making us fit for that day.

One remarkable feature of God's gift of salvation to humankind is that it does not happen apart from us. God uses aspects of our creaturely freedom as instruments of his redemptive work in our lives. It is through faith in his promise that we are made right with him. It is when we call on him for mercy that our sins are forgiven. It is as we come to him in earnest prayer that he gives us his Spirit. In short, we are required to take hold of the salvation that God has now revealed, if we would see his glory.

The argument of this book is that the rich set of closely related ideas which are here loosely summarized forms the essence of the Christian story. There are of course a number of associated themes that we have not considered. For instance, we have not examined the commission that God lays on his people to share in the mission of Jesus to the world or his equipment of them for such service with various gifts of the Spirit. But, allowing for such shortcomings and other inadequacies in presentation, these chapters claim to be a faithful sketch of the central themes of the Christian gospel. Can such a claim be justified?

Assessment

It was our intention from the beginning of this study to allow the Scriptures to speak for themselves, to set their own agenda, to disclose their own themes. Apart from the odd illustration, there has been no reference to external authorities. The aim throughout the book has been to learn from the Bible what is the nature and content of its own central message.

It would be misleading, however, to imply from this that I, as your tour guide, have approached this project without a set of theological ideas already in place. My understanding of the Scriptures has been shaped by years of study and preaching. I have also been deeply influenced by a range of theologians from the Christian tradition. Their voices are always there. It means that there is almost nothing that is original in this attempt to present afresh a classical interpretation of the gospel message. All of the arguments have already been made by significant theologians at some time in the history of Christian thought. Nevertheless, it has been my intention throughout the study to allow the Scriptures to challenge, shape and reformat those background voices, rather than to be determined by them. And doing so has opened my eyes and lit up my imagination in all sorts of ways.

Allowing the Scriptures to speak for themselves is something we learn to do in community. We learn from each other whether a certain reading of the Bible is natural or forced. Together we become more attentive to the ploys that are sometimes used to manipulate the texts to serve a particular argument or tradition. At first we tend to believe everything we are told, but over time we develop an ability to assess the integrity of those we hear or read. There is also something individual and intuitive about the discernment of what constitutes the gospel message. The Holy Spirit has been promised to lead us into all truth. There is a spark of recognition in our hearts when we are confronted with it. It has the ring of authenticity when it is presented to us. By the Spirit, we can discover for ourselves, in quite fresh ways, what is meant by it.

All this implies that only the Christian community can assess whether this short study does in some measure reflect the content of the gospel. Only the church can judge the integrity of its interpretation and the faithfulness of its presentation. Those who have not yet come under the gospel's power will always be scandalized by its claims and will struggle to make sense of its arguments. This was certainly the case when Paul proclaimed the gospel to a cultured Gentile world. It is still so when the gospel is presented today. There are certain aspects of modern religious consciousness, particularly in the West, which make it extremely difficult for those under its sway to engage unreservedly with the Christian story and be liberated by its promises. To put it bluntly, the gospel, as outlined in this study, is a cause of offence to a number of the dominant thought-forms in current religious consciousness. Three of them stand out. Let me outline them briefly.

The Scandal of Particularity

The gospel is a cause of offence to many because of its claims to exclusivity. A large number of reflective people have a deep-seated unease with the notion that Christ is the only way of salvation. It seems to them arrogant and self-conceited to offhandedly dismiss the whole range of alternative views regarding salvation that are put forward in other faiths. It is sometimes argued that once Christians found themselves in the multicultural communities of the world's great cities, and so in constant social dialogue with believers from other religions, the exclusive claims of the Christian gospel could no longer be sustained with any integrity.

Contained within these sentences are a number of significant ideas. It might be helpful to respond to some of them. First, it is implied that the exclusivity of the Christian gospel is not sustainable in a multi-faith context. The difficulty with such an argument is that the early Christians were themselves inhabitants of a multicultural world of competing faiths. Alongside the official state religion, there was the traditional pantheon of Greek and Roman gods that continued to be worshipped. Mystery religions from the East were particularly popular in the Roman military. Judaism had a strong presence in many major cities in the empire, while the various philosophical systems served the intellectual world as religions of sorts. Each craft or profession had particular religious duties and beliefs associated with it. Amid this free market of competing religious ideas, early Christians, who were an insignificantly small minority, made this startling claim regarding Jesus: 'Salvation is found in no one else, for there is no other name under heaven given to mankind by which we must be saved' (Acts 4:12).

The irony is that during the first periods of persecution, many Christians were put to death for their atheism. They did not believe in other gods. Men and women were thrown to the wild animals in the Coliseum because they refused to offer incense to the genius of Caesar. They would not acknowledge the state religion. Christianity, like its parent body Judaism, had been exclusive in its religious claims and allegiance from the very beginning. It was, however, not exclusive in its relation to others. To the amazement of all observers, it kept no one out. Rather the Christian community offered immediate, free and open access to all who would embrace the divine offer of mercy, regardless of their social status, ethnic origin, religious tradition or past lifestyle.

Second, to deny the particular or exclusive claims of the gospel is to undermine pretty much every one of the themes highlighted in this book. There are all closely linked. Most significantly, the particularity of Christ's saving work is logically dependent on the particularity of his person. The most important question to be asked is whether Jesus is indeed the only Son of God. If he is not, then any claim to the exclusivity of his saving work lacks coherence. But if he actually is, as Christians claim, the only begotten Son of the Father, then it should not surprise us that he alone is held to be the way of access into the Father's presence. 'Jesus answered, "I am the way and the truth and the life. No one comes to the Father except through me"' (John 14:6).

Third, nearly all religions seek to offer an ultimate explanation of human reality – why we are here, where we are going, how we get there. By their very nature they are logically exclusive. There can't be two final explanations of who we really are. The theory that there are many paths that lead to God is itself an overarching explanatory system, even though its beliefs about the character of God, the nature of salvation and the requirements necessary to achieve it are largely undefined. Those who hold it do not always recognize that their own all-explaining theology effectively excludes all other religions from fulfilling that role. It is not at all surprising then that those who uphold the view that there are many paths to God should be deeply offended by the exclusive claims of the Christian gospel. They are in fact competing religious systems.

The Scandal of Judgement

There is now a widespread aversion to the idea that God judges anyone. It is a common assumption today that a God who brings the past to light and deals with it appropriately in an act of judgement is somehow less noble or successful than a God who does not do so. It means that a doctrine of divine justice tends to be more of an embarrassment for many than it is a cause for praise. Among the affluent and successful of this world there is no burning desire that the truth of the past should be made known or the evil done in the dark should be brought to light and punished. It is, of course, quite different with those who have been oppressed. They long for a day of justice – a day when things will be put right. In South Africa it was those who were associated with the security organs of the state who were most opposed to the work of the Truth and Reconciliation Committee, the forum in which victims heard their oppressors confess their crimes. Those who have wielded power unfairly have so much more to lose from the exposure of the truth.

This aversion to Christ's role as Judge of all humankind is comparatively modern. For the greater part of its history, Christians have had no hesitation in affirming the words of the creed:

> On the third day he rose again;
> he ascended into heaven,
> he is seated at the right hand of the Father,
> and he will come to judge the living and the dead.[1]

Some would argue that a clearer understanding of what Jesus accomplished on the cross has brought about the theory that no one will ever come under divine judgement. But historically that is simply not true. In the sixteenth and seventeenth centuries the Western church gave its full attention to the nature of salvation and produced its finest works of reflection on the atonement. But none of the parties in the discussion denied the reality of divine judgement. The distaste for the role of Christ as the final Judge of the world is a modern phenomenon and it has come about through quite recent changes in the ways we understand our own autonomy.

The current widespread dislike for the concept of divine judgement means that many readers find themselves somewhat alienated from the multitude of Bible passages where the subject appears. Sometimes the idea of final judgement is simply blocked out of their minds when they study the Scriptures. I recently heard a man, who had been a member of a local church for many years, make the observation that Jesus did not have much to say about judgement. All those parables and all those warnings had somehow been completely filtered out of his consciousness. It was as though he had never even heard them.

Further, in the New Testament the doctrine of the atonement is in large part an answer to the human problem of sin, guilt and judgement. When the reality of divine judgement is no longer recognized, many of the biblical themes regarding redemption become superfluous. The doctrine of salvation and the redemptive message of Jesus' death lose their power to persuade and are gradually shifted to the margins of religious discussion. And there are those who believe that this is how it should be. It is no wonder that a gospel that speaks with clarity of divine judgement is a cause of offence to many a modern ear.

The Scandal of Faith

That the saving work of the triune God in our lives should be in some way dependent on the act of human believing is a scandal to many. There is no denying that the nature and possibility of faith has raised a host of difficult questions for Christian thought. Is the act of believing natural to us or is it a gracious gift of God? Can we do anything that might help us receive such faith? Does faith alone save, or has it saving power only when accompanied by a life of good works? Where is our freedom of will if God chooses us to be people of faith? Questions such as these have led to intense debates within the Western Church. However, in the vibrant discussions over the centuries on the nature of faith, all parties have recognized that human believing plays an instrumental role in salvation. On this the Scriptures were universally acknowledged as being abundantly clear.

The argument that human faith is not instrumental in salvation is also a very recent one. It seems to me that it has come about from a loss of theological nerve. The issues are deemed to be too complex, so the problem is denied. Perhaps there has also been a reaction to certain traditions where faith has been emphasized in a way that undermines the grace of God. One way or another, the gospel's emphasis on the necessity of faith in our response to the promise of the salvation has become a cause of offence in some circles.

I recognize that treating important themes such as these in a few short paragraphs right at the end of this study is rather unsatisfactory.

These are not the sort of issues which can be dealt with adequately in so brief a space. They are rather matters which need to be considered far more seriously and at far greater length than I have been able to do here.

The only defence I would make is that I have sought to present in this short book the heart of the Christian story simply, positively and in a non-combative way. It seemed to me, however, that there is some value in indicating at this final stage why it is that many thoughtful people struggle to take hold of the gospel's promises.

Further, although I have discussed these three 'causes of offence' rather hurriedly here, I have in other places given them much more detailed consideration. In a book on Christology, I have defended the uniqueness of Jesus Christ in a historical survey of the doctrine of his person. I have also sought to show, in a study on justification, the nature of the relation of salvation to divine judgement and some of the reasons why there has been a growing aversion to the concept of judgement in more recent times. And in a work on the atonement, I have argued at greater length why I believe certain popular views on the nature of salvation and the role of faith are simply inadequate.[2]

Summary

In the first chapter of his letter to the Romans Paul writes: 'I am not ashamed of the gospel, because it is the power of God that brings salvation to everyone who believes: first to the Jew, then to the Gentile' (Rom. 1:16). Paul is not embarrassed to argue against the current consensus of intellectual thought as he presents the gospel. He recognizes that the message of the cross is divinely empowered to transform, to heal and to save. It is God's way of bringing about new life, of dealing with guilt, of restoring relationships. Through it, God creates peace and establishes righteousness.

It was Paul's task, as it is ours today, to hold up the gospel in all its glory so that the world may be enthralled by its brilliance and drawn to its lustre. We are to be like the dull platinum clasp on a diamond ring, presenting the precious jewel to the light without drawing attention to ourselves. Like the clasp, we are also there to stop the gemstone from being dislodged and lost on the side of the road. Many are the forces that would seek to pry the gospel free from its position of honour and leave it neglected in the dust, an object of scorn and distaste.

Paul encourages the church in Philippi to fight for the gospel (Phil. 1:7). Each generation needs to defend again the inner logic of the Christian story and to present it afresh to the world, so that all those with eyes to see and ears to hear might discover the treasure and seek to purchase it for themselves. We can have no higher calling: 'However, I consider my life worth nothing to me; my only aim is to finish the race and complete the task the Lord Jesus has given me – the task of testifying to the good news of God's grace' (Acts 20:24).

ENDNOTES

Chapter 2. His Only Son

[1] *The Nicene Creed*.

Chapter 6. They Thought It was All Over

[1] Dietrich Bonhoeffer, *Life Together: A Discussion of Christian Fellowship* (New York: Harper and Row, 1954), pp. 118–19.

Chapter 9. Facing Up To Death

[1] John Donne, 'Death Be Not Proud' (Holy Sonnets 6), in *Selected Poetry* (ed. John Carey; OUP, 1996), p. 202.

Chapter 12. Making the First Move

[1] Francis Thompson, 'The Hound of Heaven' (stanza 1), in *An Anthology of Longer Poems* (ed. T.W. Moles and A.R. Moon; London: Longman, 1972), p. 238.
[2] Jostein Gaarder, *Sophie's World* (trans. Paulette Møller; London: Phoenix, 1998).
[3] John Donne, 'Batter My Heart' (Holy Sonnets 10), in *Selected Poetry* (ed. John Carey; OUP, 1996), p. 204.

Chapter 13. The Promise As Gift

1 Henry Adams, *Mont-Saint-Michel and Chartres* (Lexington, KY: Feather Trail Press, 2009), p. 100.

Chapter 14. Debriefing

1 *The Apostles' Creed.*
2 See Alan J. Spence, *Christology: A Guide for the Perplexed* (London: T&T Clark, 2008); *Justification: A Guide for the Perplexed* (London: T&T Clark, 2012); *The Promise of Peace: A Unified Theory of the Atonement* (London: T&T Clark, 2006), respectively.